THE AUGUSTAN REPRINT SOCIETY

THE
REFORMATION.

A

COMEDY.

(1673)

[JOSEPH ARROWSMITH]

Introduction by
DEBORAH C. PAYNE

Publication Numbers 237–238
WILLIAM ANDREWS CLARK MEMORIAL LIBRARY
University of California, Los Angeles
1986

112056

Introduction © 1986 by The William Andrews Clark Memorial Library
University of California, Los Angeles
2520 Cimarron Street
Los Angeles, California 90018

Designed and printed by The Castle Press
Pasadena, California

INTRODUCTION

THE REFORMATION seems to have passed quietly from the stage, leaving few traces beyond an edition published in 1673. From this edition we learn that the play was presented at the "Dukes Theatre" (Dorset Garden) and we know who the cast members were. But we know little about its reception and can only speculate on the date of the first performance. Even the ascription of the play to Joseph Arrowsmith, now generally accepted by scholars, is based on inference. Our only contemporary sources of information are Gerard Langbaine, that faithful recorder of Restoration drama, and John Downes, prompter for the Duke's Company during the early seventies when *The Reformation* was performed, who recorded his recollection of the play some thirty-five years later.

What biographical details we can infer about the author of *The Reformation* rest ultimately on these two sources. No author's name appears on the title page of the 1673 edition, and Langbaine lists the play in the "Unknown Authors" section of his dramatic catalogues of 1687 and 1691. He notes, however, that it is ascribed to a "Mr. *Arrowsmith*."[1] Downes says only that the author was a "Master of Arts in *Cambridge*."[2] If these scraps of information are correct, then presumably the author was Joseph Arrowsmith, of Trinity College, Cambridge, the only Arrowsmith listed in *Alumni Cantabrigienses* who fits the qualifications. Joseph Arrowsmith had become a fellow of Trinity College in 1668 and an M.A. in 1670 and was ordained in 1675.[3] That he was also a playwright in his youth is confirmed in the commonplace book of one John Watson, who identifies him as the author of a now lost comedy, *All Is Mistaken*, "acted before the King Charles 2nd Octob. 4, i67i."[4] While the ascription of *The Reformation* to the same author must remain somewhat tentative, circumstantial evidence argues strongly in its favor.[5]

[iii]

Unfortunately, no record has come to light that would allow us to date Arrowsmith's second play with the precision that we can his first. *The London Stage* posits "a late spring or early summer production" for the year 1673, on the basis of the publication date.[6] Robert Hume, though, suggests that "a *première* anything up to fifteen months earlier seems likely, given the play's topical nature."[7] As Hume points out, *The Reformation* "is a systematic debunking of Dryden, and of *Marriage A-la-Mode* in particular,"[8] a play that he and David Rodes have convincingly argued first appeared in late November or early December 1671.[9] Allusions to two other contemporary plays prove to be no help in further specifying the date of the premiere. The prologue warns the audience not to expect that "*Tartuffe or Scrupple [Scruple] should appear . . . 'tis the other house, you've lost your way.*" Tartuffe presumably refers to the principal character in *Tartuffe; or, The French Puritan* by Matthew Medbourne (who played Lysander in *The Reformation*); Scruple shows up as a character in John Wilson's comedy *The Cheats*. While such references to the repertory of the rival King's Company would make sense only if they were timely, *The London Stage* does not record performances of either play in 1672 or 1673.

Whether *The Reformation* survived long enough to bring its author any benefits we do not know. Langbaine in his 1691 *Account of the English Dramatick Poets* pronounces it "a very good Comedy" (546) but says nothing of its fate. Downes, writing seventeen years later, is somewhat more informative, if less charitable: "The Reformation in the Play, being the Reverse to the Laws of Morality and Virtue; it quickly made its Exit, to make way for a Moral one" (*Roscius Anglicanus*, 33). One suspects that Downes's explanation in 1708 for the play's demise is colored by changing tastes in comedy, but there is little reason to doubt that it died an early death.[10]

The question might arise here as to why such seemingly obscure bones should be exhumed at all. Several reasons can be offered. For the student of the theater, *The Reformation* affords a glimpse into the kind of risk the Duke's Company was willing to take on an unknown playwright, so powerful was the company's drawing power in the 1670s.[11] For the scholar of Restoration culture, the play provides a number of topical references to the Royal Society, language-planning schemes, and religious enthusiasts, not to mention contemporary English mores. For feminist critics, *The Reformation* offers a surprisingly sympathetic perspective on women, especially given the misogynist nature of many Restoration comedies.[12] Perhaps most important, though, is the interest the play holds for students of Dryden. Like its lampooning predecessor, *The Rehearsal* (1671), this comedy pokes fun at Dryden's poetic manifestos and practices of the late 1660s and early 1670s. While *The Reformation* lacks Buckingham's verve and meta-theatrical sleight of hand, in its meandering, offhand way the play still proves a worthy adversary to Dryden's *Marriage A-la-Mode*, its primary opponent in the skirmish.

All of these elements commingle to create an effective satire, one which maintains a conservative stance on art, religion, and the relations between the sexes. Satire by its very nature assumes that tradition is to be upheld and that innovation, be it in reforming men or manners, is just plain bunk. And so it is for Arrowsmith. Even the play's title cues us to his satiric intent. Arrowsmith appears to have used Melantha's remark to Palamede in *Marriage A-la-Mode* as inspiration for the name of his play: "I suppose, Sir, you have made the *Tour of France*; and having seen all that's fine there, will make a considerable reformation in the rudeness of our Court. . . ."[13] The epilogue to *Marriage A-la-Mode* expands this notion of refining the court to encompass the entire English nation, which can be — given the proper education by Dryden — led "all the way to Reformation."

Clearly, Arrowsmith wants nothing of it. The "blessed community" (act 5, scene i, line 351) blithely proposed and quickly abandoned by the four comic lovers at the end of *Marriage A-la-Mode* becomes the "Royal society of . . . Reformers" (16) in the hands of Arrowsmith. This device yields what little plot there is: some young gallants in Venice propose to free their women from the tyranny of husbands and fathers. All of them, of course, are to be self-styled reformers in a society devoted to free love and good times. To make certain that his audience grasps the not-so-veiled application to contemporary English life, Arrowsmith makes the connection explicit through the character Pacheco:

> Next, as a thing that's very much conducing to the *Reformation*, I undertake to regulate and be the pattern of all fashions in the town. To further which my Secretary shall dispatch and keep a correspondence with our beloved pattern *England*. (36)

Both Arrowsmith and Dryden bring their plays to equally chaste conclusions — for Arrowsmith's young lovers, marriage, and for Lysander and Juliana, the only married couple in the play, a legal separation. In the interim *The Reformation* manages to pass judgment on a number of topics.

Foremost among these is the state of art in England, or, to be more precise, the Dryden and the Howard manifestos circulating in any number of prefaces, essays, and dedications. Arrowsmith appears especially piqued at the Dryden and Howard assumption that modern innovations in letters are preferable to traditional genres and poetic techniques.[14] He draws the battle lines immediately in the prologue, declaring of himself in the third person that

> *He was for plodding in the Antient way:*
> *Yet he would, if this did not please our Friends,*
> *In Rime and Non-sence strive to make amends.*
> *If we procur'd Noise, Clothes, Scenes, Songs and Dance,*
> *His Siege, or Conquest he can have from* France.
> (Lines 17–21)

Arrowsmith's main weapon in this literary skirmish is his character of the Tutor, an Englishman newly come to Venice and quickly made the guiding spirit for this society of reformers. It is, without a doubt, yet another satiric portrait of Dryden, executed in much the same spirit as Bayes in *The Rehearsal*.[15] While the Tutor lacks the verbal tics and physical mannerisms which made Buckingham's creation so memorable, nevertheless he remains very funny indeed. More important, he becomes a useful vehicle, especially in act 4, scene 1, for Arrowsmith to mock several of Dryden's poetic principles.

In this scene the Tutor offers up a recipe for writing heroic

drama to his young reformers (all of whom comment sardon-
ically on each rule in a series of asides, thus providing a
"normative" reaction for the audience to identify with). The
Tutor's remarks here appear to be a pastiche of Dryden criticism: a pinch of the dedication to *Marriage A-la-Mode*, a dash
of *An Essay of Dramatick Poesy*, even a sprinkling of the preface to *An Evening's Love*. For instance, Dryden's criticism in
Dramatick Poesy of the English dramatic tradition comes un-
der fire when the Tutor acknowledges grudgingly that

> we have some three or four, as *Fletcher, Johnson, Shakespear,
> Davenant*, that have scribled themselves into the bulk of follies
> and are admired to, but ne're knew the laws of heroick or
> dramatick poesy, nor faith to write true English neither. (47)

Additionally, the Tutor's unwitting comments expose the
more pronounced excesses of heroic drama; he declares to the
young reformers that they need simply take

> some three or four or half a dozen Kings . . . two Ladies in Love
> with one man . . . a Hero that shall fight with all the world . . .
> a dancing singing ghost or two . . . put your story into rime, and
> kill enough at the end of the Play, and *Probatum est* your business
> is done for Tragedy. (48)

Finally, Dryden's characteristic profession of modesty, particularly in regard to his writing of comedy, is mocked ("Then
as for Comedy, which I was saying my Genius does not lead
me to" [48]), as is his penchant for holding forth in coffee-
houses (49).

This is all fairly predictable stuff, and Arrowsmith, even
given his inexperience as a playwright, does not display much
dramaturgical common sense. As opposed to *The Rehearsal*,
where the excesses of heroic drama are enacted in that daft
little play within a play so that we experience the genre at its
most ludicrous, *The Reformation* contains too many parodic
speeches to be truly effective theater. It is the old distinction
between showing and telling, and, unfortunately, *The Reformation* tells and tells.

What elevates the play above local literary squabbles is

Arrowsmith's conviction that literary innovation as practiced by Dryden et al. results from a pervasive obsession in Restoration society with the newfangled (thus the many derogatory topical references to virtuosi, French fashion, and modish life).[16] To combat this alarming trend, Arrowsmith associates literary and sexual reformation with the political and religious reformations of the Interregnum, a period of English history the audience presumably does not want to repeat. In act 2, scene 1, Antonio, reflecting on the reformers' new society, quips that "this may make us as famous, as inventing a new Religion" (20). Furthermore, one of the stanzas of the lyric Antonio's boy sings makes the connection even more explicit:

> *Away with all things that sound like to Laws,*
> *In this our new* Reformation;
> *Let the Formalists prate, the good old cause*
> *Is a general toleration.*
> *From this time they're free*
> *A veyl's Heresie*
> *And a Vizard Excommunication.*
>
> (19)

Predictably, the young lovers, by preferring marriage to "general toleration," become respectable "Formalists" once again, returning to the traditional institutions Arrowsmith upholds. As for the Tutor, he is sworn by the reformed reformers "to produce a Play which shall have nothing in't borrow'd, nor improbable, nor prophane, nor bawdy" (79).

Whether or not contemporary audiences found *The Reformation* dramatically satisfying, they would have been intimately familiar with the targets of Arrowsmith's humor and thus able to appreciate every nuance of his satiric thrusts. But what of modern audiences? At first glance, *The Reformation* would seem to offer lightweight entertainment to an audience accustomed to situation comedies based on similar premises (the basic plot line — rebellion and partying among young people before they are reabsorbed into the social structure — is the stuff of teenage movies). Some charming scenes stand out: Lysander clowning with his mistress, Aemilia, or Juliana instructing her young cousin in the ways of men.

Several speeches by women about their lot in life seem peculiarly modern in tone. The two young sisters, Ismena and Mariana, make a number of passing comments on the feminine condition: "'Tis the mens interest to keep us thus enclose'd," or "'Tis strange the very being women should oblige us to dissemble thus" (10, 66). But Arrowsmith is no Bathsua Makin. The women's complaints are whisked away like everything else in the overly tidy plot. Unhappily, we must conclude that even given the recent trend in reviving obscure plays (the London production of *Wild Oats* comes to mind), *The Reformation* has little to offer playgoers. Arrowsmith lacks dramatic flair, and the play's topicality would be a serious problem for a modern audience. The very thing which makes for interesting scholarship in this instance makes for poor theater. Unless like Brecht we want our audience poised with flashlight over footnotes, it would be difficult to imagine even academics enjoying this play in the performance. Reading it, though, is another matter.

The American University
Washington, D.C.

NOTES TO THE INTRODUCTION

I would like to thank Robert D. Hume, David S. Rodes, and Nancy M. Shea for their many generous comments and suggestions. I would also like to thank James A. Winn for allowing me to see relevant typescript pages from his forthcoming biography of Dryden.

1. See Gerard Langbaine, *Momus Triumphans* (London, 1688 [1687]), 31, published in facsimile as ARS no. 150; *A New Catalogue of English Plays* (London, 1688 [1687]), 31; and *An Account of the English Dramatick Poets* (London, 1691), also published in facsimile by ARS as special publication no. 5 (2 vols.). *An Exact Catalogue of All the Comedies, Tragedies, Tragi-Comedies, Opera's, Masks, Pastorals and Interludes* (Oxford, 1680), whose editorship is attributed to Langbaine, does not list an author for *The Reformation*; see Hugh Macdonald, *John Dryden, a Bibliography of Early Editions and of Drydeniana* (Oxford: Clarendon Press, 1939), 222, item 197.

2. *Roscius Anglicanus* (London, 1708), 33, also published in facsimile as ARS no. 134.

3. *Alumni Cantabrigienses*, pt. 1, comp. John Venn and J. A. Venn, 4 vols. (Cambridge: Cambridge University Press, 1922–27), 1:42. His son, listed as Joseph Arrowsmyth, was also admitted pensioner at Trinity.

4. This lost comedy is described (but not named) by Harold Love in *Notes and Queries*, n.s. 14, no. 6 (June 1967): 217–18; see esp. 217 n. 2. Judith Milhous and Robert D. Hume identify the title in "Attribution Problems in English Drama, 1660–1700," *Harvard Library Bulletin* 31 (1983): 9.

5. To these two dramatic offerings we can probably add at least one other literary endeavor, *The Life of Paulus Emilius*, "English'd from the Greek: By Mr. Joseph *Arrowsmith*, late Fellow of *Trin. Coll. Camb.*," for *Plutarchs Lives. Translated From the Greek by Several Hands*, 5 vols. (London, 1683–86), 2:179–248. A broadside, *The Loyal Martyrs* (London, 1700?), is assigned, rather improbably, to Joseph Arrowsmith in Donald Wing, comp., *Short-Title Catalogue*, rev. ed., vol. 1 (New York: Modern Language Association of America, 1972), A3779. The *British Museum Catalogue*, however, merely attributes it to an Arrowsmith, "*Traveller*"; the full title indicates that this Arrowsmith and his wife were captives of the Spanish Inquisition and "condemned to be burnt alive"!

The *National Union Catalogue, Pre-1956 Imprints* also attributes to Joseph Arrowsmith an 1815 "comic interlude, in one act" (29 pages). The interlude is included in volume 63 of Fawcett's collection of eighteenth- and nineteenth-century English drama, but nowhere in the collection is any attribution made to Arrowsmith. The interlude itself bears scant resemblance to the original text and could scarcely be considered an adaptation of Arrowsmith's play.

6. *The London Stage, 1660–1800*, pt. 1, *1660–1700*, ed. William Van Lennep (Carbondale: Southern Illinois University Press, 1965), 205. The play is listed for 24 November 1673 in *The Term Catalogues, 1668–1709*, ed. Edward Arber, 3 vols. (London, 1903–6), 1:152. Such a listing is not, however, a reliable.guide to performance date; see Judith Milhous and Robert D. Hume, "Dating Play Premières from Publication Data, 1660–1700," *Harvard Library Bulletin* 22 (1974): 374–405.

7. *The Development of English Drama in the Late Seventeenth Century* (Oxford: Clarendon Press, 1976), 292 n. 2. Hume points out that *The Reformation* "must have been acted by August 1673, when Philip Cademan (who played Pedro) was injured" (ibid.). See also Milhous and Hume, "Dating Play Premières," 388.

8. *Development*, 292. James A. Winn, *John Dryden and His World* (Yale University Press, forthcoming), detects additional satire directed at Dryden's subsequent comedy, *The Assignation*, which he believes was on the stage by early fall 1672. If Winn is correct on both counts, this information would help in dating *The Reformation*, but the satiric advice in the passage that he cites (see *Reformation*, 48) seems to me to be general to Restoration comedy and heroic drama rather than specific to *The Assignation*.

9. Robert D. Hume, "The Date of Dryden's *Marriage A-la-Mode*," *Harvard Library Bulletin* 21 (1973): 161–66; and Rodes, Commentary to *Marriage A-la-Mode*, in *The Works of John Dryden*, vol. 11, ed. John Loftis and David Stuart Rodes (Berkeley and Los Angeles: University of California Press, 1978), 460.

10. The *BMC* lists "another edition" of the play in 1683 (Wing, A3781), which could indicate a revival in the early eighties. No such revival, however, is listed in *The London Stage*.

11. Robert Hume offers an especially comprehensive overview of the fortunes of the two companies during this decade; see *Development*, 280–339, esp. 280–99.

12. Susan Staves notes that even "so undistinguished a writer as Joseph Arrowsmith treats with some seriousness secondary married characters like Lysander and his unfaithful wife Juliana in *The Reformation* (1673)"; see *Players' Scepters: Fictions of Authority in the Restoration* (Lincoln: University of Nebraska Press, 1979), 161.

13. *Works of John Dryden*, 11:244.

14. See, for instance, Edward Howard's preface to *The Womens Conquest: A Tragi-Comedy* (1671), where he asserts both the primacy of the moderns and the superiority of rhyme over prose:

> ... he were weakly an admirer of times past, that by an over dotage on them, would continue himself in a Childhood of knowledge.
> ... it is plainly to be observed, that generally Men write better for the Stage this way, (I mean in Rhime) then they have, or can do, after the manner of our former Poets without it. . . . (Sigs. A2v, A4v)

15. James O. Halliwell, *A Dictionary of Old English Plays* (London: John Russell Smith, 1860), remarks that "in part, this comedy appears like a second Rehearsal against Dryden" (207); and Hugh Macdonald, *John Dryden*, 207, item 180, notices that "the play (pp. 47–8) contains an amusing burlesque of Dryden's methods." Robert Hume, *Development*, 292, compares the play to *The Rehearsal*. John Harrington Smith in *The Gay Couple in Restoration Comedy* (Cambridge, Mass.: Harvard University Press, 1948) makes the rather odd observation that the Tutor is a personation of Wycherley (139 n. 13), an unlikely application. James Winn, *John Dryden and His World*, notes that an even earlier incarnation of Dryden is to be found in the character of "Drybob" in Shadwell's *The Humorists* (first performed 10 December 1670). Both Bayes and the Tutor bear resemblance to this "Fantastick Coxcomb."

16. Dane Farnsworth Smith, *Plays about the Theatre in England from "The Rehearsal" in 1671 to the Licensing Act in 1737* (London: Oxford University Press, 1936), also notes that "the discussion which accompanies [the reformers'] efforts in behalf of the lovers brings out the fact that in England affairs of the heart have fallen into excessive licence, and that this licence is also reflected in the literature of that country" (38).

BIBLIOGRAPHICAL NOTE

The Reformation. A Comedy (1673) is reproduced from the copy in the Clark Library (Shelf Mark: *PR3316/A64R3). Because of creases on pages 49, 55, and 56 of the Clark copy, those pages are substituted here from a copy in the Folger Shakespeare Library (Shelf Mark: A3780). A typical type page (7) measures 186 x 110 mm. Gertrude L. Woodward and James G. McManaway, *A Check List of English Plays, 1641-1700* (Chicago: Newberry Library, 1945) record two issues of the 1673 edition, one with a winged head and the other with a floral ornament on the title page (items 983 and 984).

THE
REFORMATION.
A
COMEDY.
ACTED
At the
Dukes Theater.

By Mr. Arrowsmith

Sunt, quibus in Satyra videor nimis acer ----
Horat. lib. 2. Sat. 1.

LONDON,

Printed for *William Cademan*, at the Popes-Head, in the
Lower walk of the New *Exchange* in the *Strand*.
MDCLXXIII.

PROLOGUE.

I Smile to think how every One that's here,
Expects Tartuffe or Scrupple should appear;
Who with Religions Twang and Mouth a-splay
Should Conventicle now instead of play :
But 'tis the other house, you've lost your way.
Here's nothing like a holy Reformation,
Nor Drum, nor Trumpet, though so much in Fashion
In all admired Playes of th' new Translation.
Nay can you Guess what our dull Rogue should mean?
He ha's not left us Room for Gaudy Scene;
Which uses to amuse you for a time,
Whil'st Non-sence safely glides away in Rime.
I'le swear I had advis'd him for the best,
To Lard it with fat Song or bawdy jeast
Or write in Verse and huffe the Gods at least.
But he was humoursome and bid me say,
He was for plodding in the Antient way :
Yet he would, if this did not please our Friends,
In Rime and Non-sence strive to make amends.
If we procur'd Noise, Clothes, Scenes, Songs and Dance,
His Siege, or Conquest he can have from France.

Dramatis Personæ.

Camillo an old severe Father.   *Mr.* Samford

Pacheco his Son a fop and a reformer.   *Mr.* Ant. Leigh

Tutor to Pacheco an English-man.   *Mr.* Underhil

Antonio ⎫ Reformers.   ⎧*Mr.* Harris.

Pedro   ⎭   ⎩*Mr.* Cademan

Leandro in love with Ismena.   *Mr.* Cosby

Lysander Husband to Juliana.   *Mr.* Medbourne

Pisauro Gallant to Juliana a Reformer. *Mr.* Smith

Boy to Antonio.

Mariana ⎫ daughters to Camillo.   ⎧*Mrs.* Caff.

Ismena   ⎭   ⎩*Mrs.* Johnson.

Juliana wife to Lysander.   *Mrs.* Batterton

Lelia Cozen to Juliana.   *Mrs.* Osborn

Æmilia Mistriss to Lysander.   *Mrs.* Lee

Nurse.   *Mrs.* Norris

Lucia Servant to Æmilia.

Scene Venice.

THE
REFORMATION.

ACT I.   SCENE I.

Antonio.   Pedro.

Ant. BUT that I know thee honeft, I could not guefs
thou had'ft a lefs defign, than the betraying of
this Town of *Venice* to the Grand Seignior.

Ped. Or, fince thou haft fuch an opinion
of my honefty, what do'ft thou think of the retaking *Candy?*

Ant. In earneft *Pedro,* thou haft been as mufing this two
hours, as a Polititian would be thought to be, when he
thinks of juft nothing; fometimes you ftand crofs arm'd, or bi-
ting of your nails; by and by nod, as it it was concluded:
then on the fudden fcratch your head, as if fome prodigious
accident had ruin'd the conqueft of the *Indies.*

Ped. I am pleafed it affords you mirth *Antonio.*

Ant. What a Divel ayl'ft man? if it be want of Wench
or Money, (as I'me fure thou can'ft haye no other caufe of
Melancholy) thou haft lived long enough, one would think,
to purchafe confidence to tell thy Friend.

Ped. Thou'rt fure to guefs right, without being thought a
Conjurer, nay you might have left one of them out too, for

Heaven fend me money, and i'le never throw away a thought, on any thing that's Woman ; whilft I know how to purchafe them from a Ducat upwards.

Ant. But it may be you are grown particular; I have known as brawny a Donn as your Worfhip, that has fhrunk to the thinnefs of a Bul-rufh, in lefs than two months time, for this thing cal'd Woman, that you talk of.

Ped. Certainly thou haft a better opinion of my under-ftanding ; particularly as the world goes now ? Why *Antonio*, I tell thee, I will fooner turn Pimp to a Suburb Bawdy Houfe, where there is nothing to be got, but blows, dead Wine, and the Pox: or Hermit, and forfwear the fight of them, another extream, and as great a punifhment, as------

Ant. Not fo fierce, good *Pedro*, it muft be money then.

Ped. Yes faith, I was thinking, fince my Father will not be fo civil as to dye, what I fhall do to live.

Ant. He begins to grow a little rude now, that's the truth on't, I had one , thank my Fortune, that came to his Eftate betimes, kept it till his Leafe of one and twenty Years was run out, and never thought good to renew.

Ped. That was kind, but mine's fourfcore, yet thinks as little of Death, as he did at fifteen : and o' my confcience is as far from it ; nay that that vexes me I can't reft for his rules of temperance, and I know not what, and how he lived when he was a young man.

Ant. Pox o' their Morals, when they are once paft plea-fures themfelves, they envy us. They ne're confider fhould we all live, as they do now, the World would be undone, I tell thee *Pedro* , if it were not for this debauchery, that kicks up our heels in convenient time, it would not hold half of us.

Ped. It would be pleafant, but to hear what cunning con-trivances I had to live in my Melancholy fit.

Ant. Will you give me leave to guefs ? I'le lay my life gaming was the firft propofal.

Ped. Right, and concluded on, till I confidered there was never a Scriveners Clerk, or Taylors Prentice about the
Town,

Town, but underftood the trade; nay more, the very VVomen get it, and cheat with as much confidence as a Hec. that has but one ftake left, fo that defign was ruin'd: my next was a Souldiers Life.

Ant. The certain retreat of a broken Gamfter.

Ped. But methoughts it was a little undecent for a man of my Quality, to walk the Street with one Leg, it may be never an Arm, and half a Nofe.

Ant. Thou never thinkeft how people would be concern'd for thee; one that fo proper a Gentleman fhould not be able to carry his Drink to his Head, the Women that your dancing was fpoiled; befides the Honor Man.

Ped. Pox on't, That fignifies juft as much as Peoples Pitty, when one's certain of hanging: I'le have none on't: next I was for Poetry.

Ant. Why what could put that into thy Head? that's the high way to Beggary.

Ped. Not as the World goes now: Befides, believe me, it is an eafie Trade to one that underftands a modern language or two, and will tranflate.

Ant. Nay hee muft rime too, or the Ladies wil nere be pleas'd.

Ped. Phu! That's but a weeks practice at *Crambo*, and once obtain'd faves us pains: for 'tis impoffible to write non-fence in't, fome few long words, and half a fcore fentences out of *Seneca*'s Tragedies, make an Heroick Poet.

Ant. Come, thou haft more wit than to think on't, never trouble thy felf, thou fhalt want nothing whilft thy Father lives; and when he dyes, I know it all fecure.

Ped. You are ftill my Friend. That that vext me was to fee that Rogue *Pifauro,* thrive by Air, wear his Jewels, variety of Cloths, keep his Lacquais, Horfes, play as deep as any man, and all this out of nothing.

Ant. It muft be fome Woman, the little Rogues are grown fo loving fince thefe Wars, and want of men, that they begin to take it ill to be courted, and provide for themfelves.

Ped. I

(4)

Ped. I could nere difcover't, he's as private as a Con-
feffor.

Ant. And upon the fame account, for he gets money to
conceal her vices: nay your Conteffor is like him too in this,
that he feldome hides the Womens faults, but in the fame
time he faves his own credit. But if it be a Woman, much
good may it do him, I fhall never envy him.

Ped. Nor I, He had better thrafh, or be chain'd to the
Gallyes.

Ant. No more, here he is.

Enter Pifauro.

Pif. Save ye Gallants, I interrupt you.

Ped. No *Pifauro*, we were juft now gueffing how thou
did'ft to live.

Pif. Faith Gentlemen ye are both my Friends, but we
Chymifts always conceal our great fecret by which we thrive.

Ped. Heaven fend the Furnace where you make your gold,
don't prove too hot for you.

Ant. But why in this Garb? thou ufeft to outfhine the
Sun.

Pif. I am forry Gentlemen you have hit upon two Qu fti-
ons, I muft be fo uncivil as not to anfwer; but hereafter
when things grow ripe.

Ant. There needs no excufe *Pifauro*.

Pif. Your defign goes forward with *Pacheco*?

Ant. Yes, yes I intend to carry *Pedro* thither,

Pif. And 'tis odds but I'le bring a Friend.

Ant. Doft think the Women will come in?

Pif. Nere fear't they'l not ftand out at any thing that
makes for pleafure.

Ped. Thefe are myfteries Gentlemen.

Ant. I'le unriddle all as we go.

Pif. Wee'l all meet anon, for the prefent I muft leave
you, and to a patient, though I think he is paft cure.

Ant. What's his Difeafe prethee, that thou art turn'd Quack?

Ped. The Gentile one i'le warrant you, he cures that by
his own experience.

Pif. No

Pif. No Faith worfe, he's taken o'th' fudden with a love frenzy, and runs mad for a Wench.

Ant. Pox on him, get him one then.

Pif. That will not do, I have offer'd him as fair as any one, but he is come to his Sonnets, and Serenades, fighs and walks with his Hat over his Eyes in deep meditation of doggrell love verfes, calls her by fine Romantick names, fometimes fhe is *Celia* fair, then *Phyllis*, *Amarillis*, *Clelia*, and the Devil and all, but her right name, and that I am now going to learn.

Ped. Prethee give him a little Ratsbain, or fome cold Poyfon to cool his pluck; in love; I thought the World had learn't more witt above this 12 month.

Ant. May we know the man?

Pif. I'le try but one Medicine more, and if that cure not, deliver him over to be baited : In the mean time if you chance to guefs, pray conceal it till the game grows hot. Gallants adieu.

Ant. Adieu *Pifauro.* Come *Pedro* you won't fail.

[*Exeunt.*

Scena Secunda..

Enter Juliana.

Jul. I wifh fhe were return'd, for I'me impatient till I hear fome news, Heaven fend thee meet him, and me rid of this fond Husband. I am as weary of him, as a VVoman can be of a Man, fhe has married for money ; I think I hear her. *Enter* Lelia.

Oh *Lelia* did you find him? and will he come?

Lel. Yes Madam,

Jul. But art fure he faid fo? for thou art fo apt to forget.

Lel. As fure Madam as that you long for his coming.

Jul. Did'ft remember the hour too?

Lel. Lord Madam what makes you fo miftruftful? I did, if you'le have me fwear ------

Jul. No

Jul. No I believe thee, prithee Cozen pardon me, and think what a Torment 'tis to want the thing we love : Alas, now 'tis a whole long VVeek since I saw him : and besides, all the while to be troubled with a doating Husband, would make any body impatient.

Lel. Is kindness troublesome? I thought no VVoman had complain'd on that side.

Jul. O more then any t ing, from one I cannot love.

Lel. Pray Madam why did you marry then?

Jul. Poor innocent, do'st think that love's the only cause? there are a thousand stronger *Lelia*, that's the very last, in any VVomans thoughts, that's wise.

Lel. Pray instruct me then, it may be my fortune one day.

Jul. I will and dare with confidence since I know thee private. Before I married people flatter'd me, or else they thought me fair, and that little beauty *Lelia*, was the greatest of my Fortune.

Lel. and trust me Madam, a very great one too.

Jul. As it was, it proved of strength to tempt *Lysander*, who was, and still continues, one of the richest Merchants of the Town : my Parents thought the Match so great, that it vvas in vain for me to seem unvvilling : to be short, I married him, but not for love Cozen, but to maintain my Dear *Pisauro*, vvho long before had ransackt all my Virgin Treasure, and still enjoys my heart.

Lel. I shall endeavour to learn Madam.

Jul. Trust me *Lelia*, no vvay's so direct to Misery as to marry one you love. Love added to a Husbands povver, makes him perfect Tyrant ; now let him do or say his pleasure, all 's indifferent.

Lel. But is it not as much trouble Madam, to doat on your Gallant?

Jul. No *Lelia*, He has dependance on me, and all my happiness is, I know his fortune 's low ; Oh! that he were but here once dearest *Pisauro*.

Lel. Here 's your Husband Madam.

Jul. Then

Enter Lyſander.

Jul. Then I have a new Trade.　　[*ſhe weeps.*]

Lyſ. Come Deareſt, I muſt take leave ; what weeping? Thou haſt too much love.

Jul. If I had thought I could have loved ſo well, I never ſhould have married ſure, ſcarce a Week but I am left to miſery and ſolitude, methinks I could curſe him that e're invented your profeſſion.

(Aſide) Lel. Brave Woman thou ſhalt inſtruct all our Sex.

Lyſ. Chear up deareſt, 'tis but for a few days, and i'le return, and love ſtill more, if poſſible.

Jul. A day's an age to be from one I love, nay my mind give's me, you'le nere come agan, ſtay but one day.

(Aſide) Lel. Heaven ſend he does not take her at her word.

Lyſ. Fond Rogue, my word's engag'd, I cannot for a World.

Jul. No you'le nere do any thing I ask you, ſtay but one hour, come prethee do, let this beg for me.

(Aſide) Lel. Rarely acted, ſhe might deceive an Angel.

Lyſ. Wny if I ſhould thou'lt be the ſame then, and truſt me, my time is gone, nothing in the World ſhould tempt me from thee, but my credit, prethee Dear be patient.

Jul. I have no other remedy, you are always thus cruel, if you find me ſick, or dead, when you return, it will never trouble you.

Lyſ. Come prethee be not ſo unkind, thou know'ſt I love thee, thou mak'ſt me weep to hear thee talk thus.

(Aſide) Lel. Loving Cuckold ! you would have cauſe, if you knew all.

Jul. VVell if we muſt part for ever.

Lyſ. I tell thee 'tis but a day or two.

Jul. Farewel, Heaven proſper you, I muſt have the laſt look.

Lyſ. No prethee go, or elſe you hinder me. *Lelia* wait on your Miſtreſs.

Jul. One kiſs more, I'me all obedience, and then------

Lyſ. Adieu deareſt.

Jul. One

Jul. One look more. VVas't not rarely acted *Lelia?*

Lel. To the life Madam. (*Aside*)

[*Exeunt* Juliana & Lelia.

Lys. She's gone, and faith now I begin to think my self a VVretch, to abuse her thus. How easily their good nature is deceived ? Poor doating Fool! i dare swear she loves me, then why should I dissemble thus with her ? but hang't let her go, she's but a VVife, and that's enough to sully all her worth. I'le to *Emilia* and there forget her : if I can get loose, I may return a day or two the sooner for this kindness.

But when a Mistress draws, a VVife must wait.

Your Fishes alwaies choose the freshest bait.

[*Exit* Lysander.

Enter Juliana. Lelia.

Lel. He's gone Madam, He had a grievous conflict betwixt love, and business, talkt a little to himself, gave a kind look or two this way, and *Exit.*

Laughs) *Jul.* A fair riddance, Poor Fool, now he's as secure of my love , as he is of being Cuckold. VVell men may talk of their wisdom, conduct of affairs, &c. but this one VVomans vertue of dissembling, out-weighs them all *Lelia.*

Lel. True Madam, were we all as great proficients as your self.

Jul. 'Tis but getting a husband to Practice on, and thou'lt soon learn. How do I look to day Cozen?

Lel. Tempting fair.

Jul. I would be drest to all advantages, for every time I meet *Pisauro*, methinks I make a new conquest. Prethee what did he say to thee?

Lel. Hee talk't something of a *Reformation* was designd very much for our advantage, I did not well understand him; but you'l here all anon.

Jul. I wish he were here once, is't not the hour yet *Lelia*> I'le meet him, if he comes not quickly, if we chance to miss, he has the key, and knows where to expect me.

Lel. Hee'l be here Madam presently, pray be patient.

Jul. 'To

Iul. To me even time it felf does flowly move,
There's no fuch thing as patience in Love.
[E*xeunt* Juliana, Lelia.
Enter Camillo *and* Servant.

Scena Tertia.

Cam. Mariana, Ifmena, hey days! go feek'em out.
Serv. They'r not within, Sir.
Cam. Not within Sir? This 'tis! Women? I had rather have 40 Cats to look after; and they all wild too, great, wild, Hee Cats. I've feen Tygers, Lyons, Wolves coopt up, and tam'd: But let any man prove to me of his own knowledg, two Women that were fo, and i'le believe all Mandevile. O' my confcience I had all bedlams put together in me, when I got thefe girles, they make nothing of creeping through Key holes.
Ser. They'r only gone to Church Sr.
Cam. To Church Sr? what have women to do at Church Sr? can't they fay their Prayers at home, or let them quite alone, and mind their needles? I tell thee there ne're comes any good of thefe holy pretences; were I young I'de as foon marry one out of the ftewes as one of thefe religious gadders: and the truth on't is it comes much to one, for they meet with Priefts at both places. Where's *Pacheco?*
Serv. Abroad Sr.
Cam. There's a youth too, hopeful enough till this curfed voyage: if any man longs to fpoile a fon, let him fend him into *England* with an Embaffadour. They are all mad there, and hated the very true Religion, becaufe of Nunnerys and Covents, that confin'd People to Sobriety and Chaftity. I have a hopeful brood; would any thing but the down-right divel had'em.
Enter Mariana, Ifmena.

So, are you come gypfyes? not a word, I've rayl'd my felf weary at prefent, get you in, I'le but take a turn i'th'
gallery,

gallery, to recover a little, and you shall have it with a vengeance.

[Exit Camillo.

Mar. What shall we do sister, my Father's strangly angry?

Ism. Why e'ne go abroad again, and run for't, or let him talk out his talk, hee's old and quickly out of breath.

Mar. We women are most miserable creatures sister, brought up at first by some severe Parent, or kinswoman; and when we grow most sensible of bondage, deliver'd over to the tyranny of a cruel husband.

Ism. Or clap't into a nunnery to spend our lives in thinking, and contemplation, though I perswade my self there's little of religion in't: but from the small remembrance we have of men, scratch their pictures on the walls, and wish: and the first opportunity we have of being sick make use of the confessor.

Mar. Thou'rt a wild wench, will nothing tame thee?

Ism. 'Twould make a dog wild to be tyed up thus, I wonder we can never muster courage up for to rebell. I have read of women that have been famous for't, and I'm perswaded I my self have courage enough to be a general.

Mar. My Brother talkes of some design he has, I wish he would compleat it once.

Ism. Were I but a man I'de make my self renown'd in the womens quarrel, work them all deliverance; and then share the best of them.

Mar. 'Tis the mens interest to keep us thus enclos'd Ismena.

Ism. None but but a few elder brothers that are husbands *Mariana*, I dare swear were it once proposed the young rogues would dye in our defence, 'twould make their addresses cheap and easy, vvhen as novv twenty fees can scarcely purchase a good look, vvhich falls hard upon the younger brothers. You'r Melancholy Sister.

Mar. I dread my fathers anger, and the very thoughts of liberty torment me vvorse, then this imprisonment. Would my Brother vvould come home once, that vve might heare the nevvs.

Ism.

Ism. Dread! I'me asham'd to hear you name it, let's in and laugh, and weary out this tyranny.

Mar. 'Tis thy mirth that keeps me still alive.

Ism. Come wench,
   Our bodyes by a father are confin'd,
   But there's no man can rule a womans mind.

[*Exeunt Omnes.*

Scena Quarta.

Emilia. Lucia.

Emi. No news of *Lysander*?

Lu. No Madam.

pulls out her Glass. *Emi.* I have not lost my beauty yet, the same lustre sparkles in my Eyes ; and youth sits smiling on my cheeks : the same brisk heat runs through my veins, and makes me warm, and active in my love. Then why should he grow cold ? Five days and not see me ? 'tis very strange ! He's too wise to have the dotage of a wife seize him. No, 'tis another love grown happy by my ruin. I'le find out some new way to found him, for 'tis fixt. My youth must not be lost in this indifference. *Lucia* bid them bring me in a Chair and Table, and do you fetch me the Prayer-book lyes in my closet.

Luci. The Play-book Madam?

Emi. No the Prayer-book, are you Deaf?

Luci. You'd better have the other Madam, that will but make you melancholy.

Emi. Goe I say, it may be I resolve to be so.

Luci. I shall have a sad trade on't if it comes to this once. I wonder who invented these grave Books! or ever taught any of our profession to read them, I'me sure they'r very much out of our calling. *Chair and Table set out.*

Exit Lucia.

C 2

Emi.

Emi. It fhall be fo, and if this fail, I'le find fome other way to live; there are more kind men than one.

Enter Lucia, gives her the Book.

Lucia. Here Madam, but I hope you are not in earneft.

Emi. Peace Baggage, and if *Lyfander* come, tell him I'me not to be difturb'd. 〈*Sits down and turns over the Book.*

Luci. Since you are fo ferious, you fhall have none of my Company: I'le e'ne go fing a brisk fong or two i'th' next room, and blefs the firft man that comes to put you out of this humor.

Enter Lyfander.

Oh here's *Lyfander*, then I muft run for't.

(*Afide*) *Emi.* He's come, now all that's woman help me to diffemble. Yet I can find no Prayer that's fit 〈*She turns the* for me. Sure never any woman was fo wicked. 〉*book over.*

Lys. Come *Emelia* throw away thy book, and fly to my embraces, thou need'ft not ftudy any new charms. Come let me fee what 'tis that tempts thee thus: fome fmutty Novells on my life. How's this? A Prayer book! I fhould fooner expect to fee the French King turn Calvinift than to find thee in this pofture. What fad afflistion has brought thee to this mifery? Haft fpotted thy new gown? loft thy little dog? or doft want a new fafhion'd pair of Pendants? Prithee tell me.

Emi. No, No, Sr. *None* of thefe. But I have fpotted all my life, loft my innocence which you have rob'd me off; and want a new heart.

Lys. Hey day! turn'd Canter? this becomes thee worfe than fine drefs, and youthful cloths an old woman: There's fcarce a Nun will talk thus through a grate.

Emi. But I fhall when I'me there (as I refolve I will) and if I can, teach you repentance.

(*Afide*) *Lys.* Pox o' this wheadle, I fee through it, and will cure her by one as extravagant.

Emi. It is but Juft I help to wafh away your guilt, who have been the unlucky caufe.

(*Afide*)

(Aside). *Lyf.* Now for my trade. Oh *Emilia* from this minute i'me happy : give me your hand, my bloud's obedient; and I can touch thee now with as chaft thoughts, as Virgins pray.

(Aside) *Emi.* If this be real, i'me undone, but I muft on.

Lyf. Methinks I loath my former life. Oh could vve but call it back *Emilia.*

Emi. Then vve vvere bleft indeed. But fince that cannot be, I'le double all my Orifons, and that vvay make up my arrears : And never fpeak, or think of man, but vvhen I put up prayers for you, O *Lyfander.*

(Aside) ----Hang me if I can hold for laughing : if I make a good end of this, if I ever undertake to Preach again, may I turn Nun in earneft.

(Aside) *Lyf.* She will out-do me ; they have th' advantage of a voyce for whining, but I'le try. I'le to a cloyfter too, for 'tis but juft the refidue of life be fpent in punifhing this too much pamper'd flefh. There in our feveral cells we'll faft, and watch, and wafh away our guilt, and when we're fit to dye remove to heaven. Oh *Emilia* !

(Aside) *Emi.* This is counterfeit too, but how to come off I can't imagine. Well, dear *Lyfander* (for now I dare call thee fo) fince our defigns agree, let's time our Prayers, that Heaven may hear us both together.

Lyf. We'll rife before the morn.

Emi. Out-watch the pale-faced moon.

Lyf. Nor eat to fatisfie our appetite, but lengthen out our lives for our devotion.

Emi. We will not drink, but what our tears have feafon'd.

Lyf. Nor fleep. *Emi.* Nor think. *Lyf.* Nor dream. *Emi.* Nor live.

Lyf. Nor any thing but----

� They both burft *Emi.* I can hold no longer.
out a laughing. *Lyf.* Nor I by heaven. You idle rogue, could you imagine I could think thee in earneft ?

Emi. I was once half afraid that you was, till I confider'd how ill it became you.

Lyf. Now what amends for all this ? Will you never leave this jealoufie ?

Emi. You shall find that within. I did it only for to try you after your absence.

Lyf. No more of these tricks, there needs none, I am as fond as ever, come let's in and enjoy our selves, and some twenty years hence, we may venture on such a discourse in earnest. [*Exeunt.*

ACT. II. SCENA I.

Pisauro, Leandro.

Pis. YEt you resolve to have this wench?

Lea. Why I'me sure thou wouldst not have me dye, if it were only to save the trouble of praying for me.

Pis. Faith it would put me a little out of my road, that's the truth on't; but why must you needs dye? Thou hast not seen her above twice, and that at Church too: if you had been at your appointment you might have avoided such temptations; for my part I'me resolv'd to keep out of harms way.

Lea. Away you're profane.

Pis. Prithee stay till thy Saint's Canoniz'd, before thou say so; do you think it religion to kneel squinting at your mistrifs, two or three hours with your beads in your hands; and only cast up your eyes, because she's i'th' gallery above you?

Lea. Heaven made such beauty for to be ador'd.

Pis. And she'l make use of it for to be whor'd (*Aside*) Why don't you go on? I thought you had a coppy of verses on it. Heaven made &c. I shall believe you are in love, when once you talk your sublime nonsence. Heaven, Beauty, Fate, Adoration, Sun, Divinity and a few such words will make thee Poet too, and then thou'rt fit to court a Queen.

Lea. I was bewitch't to tell you, I knew you would but
mock

mock at my misfortunes; I should hardly serve *Pisaurso*.

Pis. Misfortunes do you call it? will you make me believe women can run through thee, like lightning, and set what brand upon a heart they please? Let me be thy Doctor and prescribe thee two or three of my infallible cures against this witchcraft of love. Feed high. Wench discreetly. And go to bed with a jolly cup. Probatum est --- 'tis as infallible as the Jesuites powder for a Quartan.

Lea. I see I must find some other friend to help me in my affaires. Adieu.

Pis. I'le be serious. By my troth I had such a qualm came over me once, 'twas troublesome, and lasted about a quarter of an hour, but since a she friend of mine taught me to draw the humor downward, I'me free.

Lea. I have no patience to bear this fooling.

Pis. I have done, pray pardon me; but which way do'st thou intend for to obtain her? The old man keeps her with more care, than he does his gold; He cut of a dog's ears t'other day, to search for letters: And has a gun ready charged to kill pidgeons, for fear they should be Carryers: He swounds at the sight of a post, or any thing that runs of errands.

Lea. This difficulty makes me need thy help. I know thee expert in all the tricks of women; art read in their winks and nods, canst tell how to answer with a shrug or sigh, knowst how to wheadle Chamber Maids, and make love to old nurses. Prethee be serious and advise me.

Pis. Now I see thou art in earnest, I can, and will *Leandro*.

Lea. But how dear *Pisauro*?

Pis. Why thus: old *Camillo*, Father to thy *Ismena*, has a son lately return'd from England, whither he went with our Embassador.

Lea. This way I can foresee no hopes.

Pis. Yes very much. You knew him humorsome, and conceited before his voyage; but this has added to him all the fopperies of that Nation, which they borrow from the French: so that he's the strangest piece of Fantastickness

that

that can make droll for a play: in fhort he is a meer finging fwitching Fopp.

Lea. Still you amaze me.

Pif. Suffer me. Amongſt the reſt of the Engliſh cuſtomes
'tis one, and faith almoſt the only one that pleaſes me, to
allow all poſſible freedom to their women. This he reſolves
to bring up in *Venice*, and will in ſpight of his father, begin
with his own ſiſters. There is a Royal ſociety of us, call'd the
Reformers. Doſt thou yet underſtand me?

Lea. Yes, this ſounds like ſomething.

Pif. We'l admit thee into the number, and then ſhift
for thy felf. I muſt leave you, and to the buſineſs that concerns my life (as I was telling you) my little Merchant adventures, Oh! 'tis the kindeſt thing, ſo like matrimony, and
yet no trouble. Now vve talk of reforming, could you all
thrive like me, and leave off the damn'd trade of keeping
vvenches, and let them keep you, 'tvvould be a happy vvorld.

Lea. But I'me for neither, I'me for the honeſt vvay of
marrying.

Pif. Heaven forbid, but that ſomebody ſhould like that
dull trade: for if there vvere no vvives, there vvould be no
husbands to rob to maintain us younger Brothers.

Lea. You ſtill keep your old humor; but vvhy no better
dreſt man?

Pif. I'le tell you; I ſerve her, as the vvenches uſed to ſerve
me; alvvays pretend to vvant ſomething: thou ſhalt ſee me
as glorious as the day at our next meeting.

Lea. Stay, vvho are theſe?

Enter Antonio *and* Pedro.

Pif. Antonio and *Pedro,* tvvo of the ſociety: I'le admit you
preſently.

Ped. Thou'rt a rare rogue: Hovv the Divel could'ſt thou
find Rhetorick enough to vvheadle him to this?

Ant. He did it himſelf Sir. And tells me in *England,* 'tis
thought honorable to bring their ſiſters acquainted, as they
call it, I believe ſome faſhionable name for Pimping. *'Tis
ordinary there to do it for a kinſwoman, and that may ſave a por-*
tion

tion. Heaven fend them good faces, and they never need work for their livings. Oh 'tis. ----

Pif. Save you Gallants, how does the Society go forward?

Ant. With full fail, *Pifauro.*

Pif. Shall I beg admiſſion for my friend here?

Ped. Leandro! The only man we wiſhed; but he muſt be ſworn according to form.

Lea. Your Servant Gentlemen, I ſhall willingly paſs any ceremony.

Pif. They are eaſie, only an oath or two to ſwallow, and they are gilded.

Ant. Lay your hand upon the book. 'Tis *Ovid de arte amandi,* and begin. You ſhall ſwear, to the uttermoſt of your power to reform *Venice* according to the Pattern of *Enland* in manners and diſcipline; and t at you will, without reſpeð of perſons, endeavour the extirpaticn of Tyranny, that is, the government of Husbands and Fathers, by Siſters, Aunts, Nurſes, and all other officers depending upon that Uſurpation. And that you will with the ſame ſincerity root out the ſpreading errors of Vizards, Maſques, Veyles, *Padlocks,* both for the reſtoring of loſt pleaſures to your ſelf, and the freedom of the diſtreſſed Ladys.

So help you Cupid.

Ant. So, now you are a ſworn Brother, we need keep nothing ſecret.

Pif. Where's our Grand-maſter *Pacheco?*

Ant. I left him with his Tutor, the Engliſh man, contriving which way to get his Siſters out of Priſon.

Lea. That's the Engliſh man, I warrant, that pretends ſo much to Poetry and breeding; and cenſures all the old Authors, with as much Authority as if he had been their School-maſter.

Pif. The ſame; if he gets but the upper end of a Table at an Ordinary, you ſhall have him run them over as faſt, as a Dutch-man tells money.

Ant. Sometimes he pretends to Plays too, and then he damns French, Spaniſh, and Italian in a wind, yet ſteals out

D
of

of the very worſt of them. He would be thought to have a little kindneſs for an Author or two of his own Nation, but will be ſure to ruin their reputation too, with ſome exception or other, before he leaves them.

Lea. Does he ever write himſelf?

Ant. Yes, Yes; but as all your profeſt Criticks do, damnably ill: To tell you the truth (for I have made it my buſineſs to underſtand him) the fellow has wit, but broke with driving a trade too big for his ſtock; and when *Pacheco* took him in, all he had to ſubſiſt on, was confidence, and the favour of two or three fopps.

Ped. Faith he's bravely fitted with a Maſter.

Ant. 'Tis very pleaſant to hear him talk of the advantages of this *Reformation,* his Lectures of Repartes, Converſe, Regales, and an hundred more unintelligible fopperies.

Ped. To end, he has order'd us to expect him at the old place, where we ſhall hear the Reſult of all.

Piſ. There you may expect me then an hour hence.

Ant. But how ſhall we find a Miſtreſs for *Pacheco?*

Ped. ---Why faith I have a wench I grow ſomething weary of, he ſhall have her.

Lea. No, that's too cruel.

Ant. What think you of my boy finely dreſt? The rogue has a ſmooth face, and ſings well.

Piſ. Nor that neither. I have a Cozen witty and handſome, whoſe Fathers fortunes were ruin'd in our laſt wars at *Candy:* what if we ſet her up? ſhe may teach him wit.

Ped. As you can agree. But prithee, now you talk of ſinging, let *Leandro* hear the ſong you made upon the *Reformation.*

Ant. Sing boy.

SONG.

Beauty no longer ſhall ſuffer Eclipſe,
Nor jealouſie dare to confine
The power of thoſe eyes, or uſe of thoſe lips

Which

Which nothing but kindnefs defign.
Our Ladies fhall be
As frolick as we,
Nor fhall husband or Father repine.

We'el banifh the ftratagems us'd by the State
To keep the poor women in aw,
Henceforth they themfelves, fhall rule their own fate
And defire fhall be to them a law.
Thus they being free
From Padlock and Key
May with their Reformers withdraw.

Where in private we'el teach them the Myfteries of Love,
And practife that Lecture over,
Till we the fond Scruple of honor remove,
And the end of our paffion difcover.
No maid fhall complain
Or wife figh in vain
For each may be eas'd by her Lover.

Away with all things that found like to Laws,
In this our new Reformation;
Let the Formalifts prate, the good old caufe
Is a general toleration.
From this time they're free
A veyl's Herefie
And a Vizard Excommunication.

Lea. 'Tis a brisk defign, and muft needs take among the
Ladies: but are they fo free in *England* as you pretend?

Ped. Freer than you can think Sir. 'Tis mortal fin not to
know what's what at fifteen.

Ant. Fifteen! They have loft time at that age; a Maiden-
head at thirteen is as great a rarity in the country as a wolf;
now and then in fome village there may be fome ugly Mon-
fter, that holds out longer upon force, but

Pif.

Pif. In earneft *Leandro*, the foberest women there, have more freedom of difcourfe and company, than we give to a ftale Bawd, or an old Midwife at a Chriftening: And yet the men fo free from jealoufie, that you may as foon perfwade one of us to leave whoring, as them to believe their own eyes.

Ped. Nay, they are fo contrary to us, that a Vizard Mafque is a certain fign of a free booter, and nothing makes them cover their faces but impudence.

Lea. This muft needs be the fortunate Ifland, people talk fo much off.

Ant. Now after all this, make it a matter of confcience: confider the neceffity of this *Reformation*, and how damnably we have been wheadled b thefe veiles of ours. After half a years attendance, and courting of fome delicate fhape, that would tempt a Hermit in the midft of fnow, to lofe all our expectation and compliment, and when we fee the Divels face, be forced to fly, and crofs our felves for fear of lafting.

Pif. 'Tis intolerable. I tell you I refolve to fpare no body, a Vizard fha'n't pafs though it be following her Mother to the grave: nor any face be hid by a veil, though the woman be to do penance in a Church: The truth on't is, Gentlemen, there muft be no mean, rank rebellion or nothing.

Ant. At that I'me with you, and I know not but this may make us as famous, as inventing a new Religion.

Ped. There's no queftion. Thou art well read, *'tis but finding half a dozen places in our modern Reformers, to back us, and the bufinefs is done.*

Pif. This defign has fo tickled me, that I have forgot my affignation. *Leandro* I leave you to be introduced by thefe Gentlemen.

Ant. We'l all go.

Pif. My way lies here, I'le be with you prefently.

Ant. Sings.

Let your politick nodles debate
So our women be free,
'Tis nothing to him, to thee, or to me
Who governs the Church or the State.

[*Exeunt* Ant. Ped. Leandro.

[as

[as Pisauro is going out at the other door.]

Enter Juliana and Lelia Masqued.

Pis. So my adventures begin already: though two to one be odds, I must board them; Heaven send they don't prove Fire-ships.

Jul. 'Tis he. *[to Lelia]*

Pis. Nay faith Madam, no passing this way without a small Parley, and a kind look or two.

Jul. Sure you'r some stranger you'r so rude, do you know you are in *Venice*, Sir?

Pis. Yes Madam, but I perceive you don't know the most considerable news of the place. How the Divel do you two come into these Vizards that have been out of fashion these six hours?

Jul. What Sir? and the men are to wear them to cover bad faces, as the women did to save good ones?

Pis. Well said Spitfire, come, unmasque for fear I call yours in question; for were you fair, you would be proud too, and we must hire you to keep it on.

Jul. Like enough Sir, were the prize worth taking, but what shall I get by conquering you? You look as if you had nothing about you, but a Surgeons bill, and it may be a Taylours, which must be worn out with carrying in your pocket too, if it came home with your cloaths.

Pis. As I live she guesses all my treasure within a Ducatoon: Oh for some succor to relieve the forlorn hope. *(Aside.)* Nay if you once turn wit, I'le swear you'r ugly; and now I look again I see your wall-eyes, and guess the length of your nose by the shape of your Masque. Faith Madam, the men are beholden to you, that you take such care not to fright them.

Jul. Without you repent you shall pine for this, though it be spoke at random. *(Aside.)*

Lelia. This is the strangest beggar I ever heard Madam, but you use to be charitable, give him something to put him into repair, the Gentlemen has been in a Storm.

Pis. Do you begin to open too, you pispot-emptier, you
must

must be such by the old lace shoes, and respect you have to follow the fashion at a distance.

Lel. Marry come up! one had better be out of the fashion, than out at the elbows.

Jul. Methinks one of your complexion might light upon some wife, or easy fool that would buy her pleasures at the price of perriwigs, or a new suit, you have had ill fortune Sir. Prithee *Lelia* help me to abuse him.

(*Aside*) *Pis.* Worse and worse she knows me too: yet refuse me, if (except this minute to *Leandro*) I ever told it so much as to my Confessor, but most of your women are witches.

Lel. Or what do you think of a Gentleman Usher? you have a good fashionable face; and your Lady will see to bring your legs to a fit size.

Jul. No, No; I tell you he scorns any thing of Service. The Ladies doat on him, 'tis ten to one, but that hee's just now sent for, you see hee's drest for the purpose.

Pis. Pox on you both, for I have nothing left to say but curses, and they shall be home: may you be both Padlock'd, chayn'd together, and turn'd upon a Common; or which is yet worse, may you always gape for meat, and it be death for any man to feed you.

Jul. Nay if you be so good at that, I'le have one for you too; may you have nothing to maintain you, but the favor of some woman, and she grow weary and discard you.

Pis. Heaven forbid, that bites, I'de give all the world to see this Divel, and will before I go.

Jul. Nay, never take the pains to strive.

[*She unmasques her self.*]

Pis. How! *Juliana*! Could you curse with so much cruelty, when you knew me too?

Jul. Don't you deserve it? how do you like my wall-eyes now?

Pis. Now you're cruel: Good faith I did not know thee, I was just coming.

Jul. I have waited above this two hours, but you men when you once get a hank upon our affections, think you may do any thing.

Pis.

Pif. By this you fha'n't be angry. I have the pleafan'ft ftory to tell you; come be pleafed *Lelia* fhall engage for me.

Lel. Yes I have caufe, you did not abufe me ?

Pif. Peace, I'le ftop thy mouth with a husband Girle.

Lel. Say you fo? I have done.

Jul. Well I'le try you once again, but if ever ----I'le only go round and meet you, you have the key of the back door.

[*Exeunt* Juliana, Lelia.

Pif. What fool will truft himfelf to wind and waves ?
When thus he reaps the fruit and trouble faves?
A Husband's factor for his wifes Gallant,
And till he break, the other nere can want.

[*Exit* Pifauro.

Scena Secunda.

Pacheco, Tutor.

Pac. (Throws back his wig.) That was fomething nigh it, but methinks I ha'n't the right fling yet. I'le try agen.

Tut. There you nickt it. Now for your Virtuofo's Looking glafs.

Pac. Pulls out a piece of polifht mettal.)

Tut. Right Sir, that expreffes your defign of promoting new experiments. You muft obferve it in every thing not fo much as a tooth-picker, but muft have fomething extraordinary.

Pac. Would not this fhew genteel and modifh in a Play-houfe?

Tut. This and the managing your comb will make you pafs for a Critick in the fafhion. The next thing you may practice is fome few books, and then you are a wit too.

Pac. That's the only thing I aim at; on good *Tutor.*

Tut. When you come to a new Play, and know the Author is no fighter, and you may venture to abufe him; firft fit grave and unconcern'd, and be fure to caft an eye upon fome fam'd wit of the town, and take him for your pattern.

Pac. But how if there be none there *Tutor.*

Tut. Why then if any thing takes in general you may venture.

ture to fmile a little : if only amongft fome few, and you imagine it not good, caft a fcornful look about you, as if you pittied their ignorance. Above all things commend nothing without fome exception. Thefe few rules well obferv'd, you'l be a ftandard of carriage unto others.

Pac. Nay, they almoft take me for a wit already, I know all the *Poets* Chriften names; and call *Tom* and *Jack* with as much confidence, as if I had been their God-father.

Tut. That's well: There's very much in that. You may take occafion to give them the familiar fhrug, talk aloud, and fwear, *Tom* the humour in thy laft Prologue was high and new. Pox on thee for a rogue, thoul't grow famous. A whifper now and then, with a great laugh after it does well.

Pac. Did not you talk fomething of a fhrug? You promis'd to teach me the way of accofting people, that's the word I think in *England*.

Tut. Yes, mark. Firft take notice of no body in bad cloaths, or poor, though it fhould be your own Father come out of the country for to fee you: or if you muft needs fpeak to him, withdraw, and after half a fcore words return, and tell the company that a Tenant wants difpatch, or a dependant on the family; and you'l be with them prefently.

Pac. I fha'n't forget this, 'tis fo natural to me ever fince I have been in *England*. I can't tell what to fay to any one that wants a white wig, and a new fuit.

Tut. When you're nigh a perfon of honour, and one you think it a credit to be acquainted with, be fure to turn and fmile, though it be a fecret hee's whifpering to another, and you don't hear a word. This makes you be thought familiar, and a favorite at Court.

Pac. That's excellent, faith Tutor I'le remember I'le warrant you.

Tut. As for your Equals, your fhrug, or fhaking of the head, as if you had been at a debauch the night before, is creditable and modifh. As to practice: Mounfieur *Pacheco?* (fhrugs.) Come, how is't? (fhrugs) What at fome deep engagement

gagement with the Ladies laſt night, or a tavern on my life. (ſhrugs.)

Pacheco imitates him.

Tut. That's right, and confirms him, that you drink and wench, things of more credit, as the world goes, than a Knight-hood, or the command of a Regiment.

Pac. Incomparable *Tutor* ! but no more, for fear I forget : beſides I fear they ſtay for us ; and I would not hinder the *Reformation*, to be great Duke.   [*Exit* Pacheco.

Tut. In *England*, where each Writer ſhares the ſtakes,
The gains are ſmall, and one the other breaks.
But here alone without controul I rule,
His trade can't fail that's *Tutor* to a fool.
[Exit Tutor.

ACT. III. SCENE I.

Lyſander, Tutor.

Tutor. I Tell you truth Sir.
   Lyſ. *Piſauro* ? the thing it ſelf does not ſo much perplex me, as that I'me over-reacht ; and yet it cannot be ; ſhe's all fondneſs.

Tut. What greater ground can you propoſe for your ſuſpicion ? Conſider Sir, had you the ſame deſign what other way is left to hide it ? But I have done the office of a friend believed or not.

Lyſ. This argument has convinced me, and ſince thou art ſo much my Friend, I'le tell you; I have the ſame deſign, and love a Miſtreſs more than twenty Wives, and by this very means conceal it from her. But People that pretend themſelves to cunning, ſeldom ſee through others. Doſt think he's there now ?

Tut. I'me ſure he was Sir within this half hour I ſee him enter.

E
Lyſ.

Lyf. Then I will furprize them. I know fhe can't expect me yet a day or two. I'le only difpatch an houres bufinefs and be with them. Pray accept of this acknow-

Gives him gold. ledgment, you're far from home and truft me 'tis a real kindnefs. For had I found it out my felf I know not what a fudden heat might drive me to. A little time to pawfe will make me unconcern'd.

Tut. If this project chance to fail, within a day or two I'le find out one that fhall be certain.

Lyf. Till my one eyes convince me I'le be ftill the fame. Adieu.

[*Exit* Lyfander.

Tut. Your Servant Sir. Thus far things go well, and here's a good reward. But let me think. This Gallant keeps his Miftrifs too. That fhall to *Juliana.* And fince they are fo much for *Reformation* I'le fhow them one more of our Country tricks. The taking fees on both fides.

[*Exit* Tutor.

ACT III. SCENE II.

Mariana, Ifmena.

(*as at work.*)

Ma. THis *England* muft be a blefled place my Brother talks fo much of it.

If. Would I were there; that I might be acquainted with thefe men, I have fuch a tickling runs through me when I fee them.

Ma. And there it is commoner for them to go to a treat, than for us to go to Church; never a day but this Lords or that Knights Coach waits on you and hurrys you to a Play, thence into the Park, then there's fuch perpetual Mafquerades and Balls, that 'tis Carnival all the year.

If. And here if we have a little liberty before Lent we are fure to pine for't, fo that the whole year fcarce recruits us again.

Mar.

Mar. They have no such thing there: they account it almost sin not to eat flesh when 'tis forbidden by the Church.

If. That's a life worth something, I wonder why these old men live, sure there they all dy when they're young, or else the women never knew their Fathers, for my part I wish I had never known mine : I'me sure he's grievous troublesome.

Ma. Fie *Ismena* consider he is your Father.

If. Fie me no fies, *Mariana*, I vvonder vvho disturbs his telling of money, or any thing he has a mind to: does he think because he had the pleasure to get us, vve are bound to be his Slaves? if he had not been my Father 'tis odds but somebody else vvould, I've heard them say my Mother vvas a handsome vvoman.

Mar. Peace for shame and be content a vvhile, you knovv vvhat my Brother promised us to day.

If. I vvish he vvould make his vvords good and bring them once. But I have a strong fancy vve shall quarrel, for I have had a mind to every man I have seen yet.

Mar. I vvish it vvere come to that once, for I am grievous weary of vvorking these vertuous Stories of constant vvives.

If. Constant! thine I think's *Penelope* an old withered witch that was forced to spin ten years to earn money to pay her drudges with; and when she had wearied them all out, sent to seek her Husband; mine's *Lucretia*, it may be she was vertuous but it would never grieve one to kill ones self, so one was well ravished first.

Ma. Now thou art stark mad.

If. Phu! we may say any thing amongst our selves, if we did not talk merrily how should vve be able to live?

Mar. Heark, I hear my Father, Heaven send him in a better humor than vvhen he last left us.

If He'd best look to himself, for such another Scold vvould cut off tvvo or three years at least.

Enter Camillo *and* Nurse.

Cam. So, this I like, if I ever catch you abroad again vvithout my leave, do you hear I'le have your legs tyed together.

Ism. We may fometimes go to Church Sir.

Cam. No, I'de rather have thee ftay at home and be damn'd; I wonder what 'tis you do at Church make mouths at fome young fellow, who talks to you all the while on his beads. Come come, I know all your tricks and will have you ftay at home; nor fhall any come to fee you, no not your Brother to tell you Stories of his *England* voyage : curfe on the Nation.

Ma. Not my Brother Sir ? this is too fevere.

Cam. No not your Brother *Minks*; you're like to come to good when you'l be inftructing of your Father. Here *Nurfe* take the Keys, and give no more liberty than the two next rooms affofd without my order.

Nurfe. I warrant you Sir, I'le keep them clofe.

[*Exit* Camillo.

Now Mrs. *Ifmena* I fhall be even with you for all your f.umps.

They fhake her.

Ism. Nay as long as you are with us we fhall want no fport, come Sifter help me to fhake her to pieces.

Nurf. Will you murder me? Oh!

Mar. The other fhake does it, I heard her bones rattle.

Nurf. Oh I am dead.

Mar. You keep them clofe you old toadftool! thou art too ugly to be a Bawd.

Ism. She had been a Witch Sifter, but that the Divel loathed to fuck her.

Nurf. When you are once in your pound I'le make you faft for this, you fha'n't fo much as fee a man this twelve-moneth, nay, I'le have your hands tied behind you, that you may not fcratch where it itches.

Ism. That would be hard indeed Sifter.

Mar. Leave your threats, or you know your old punifh-ment: or what do you think of toffing her in a blanquet ? fhe's fo old and dry fhe muft be light.

Ism. Excellent! if we had her in the Garden on a windy day 'twould be a fure riddance; But now I think on't Sifter

weel

we'l get fome packthread and fly her as the boyes do a paper kite with a Candle and Lanthorn at her tayl. She'l make a rare Comet.

Mar. 'Tis the beft ufe of her, fhe's like the picture of one of the Sibylls above in the Dining room, and this is the way to make her prophecy.

Nurf. Well Mrs. *Percks* this goes to your Father, with fome improvement of my own.

Mar. If you dare Keeks, we'l in and ftudy a revenge.

Ifm. Farewell Rattle, and be fure to keep us clofe.

Shakes
her.
                       [*Exeunt* Mariana, Ifmena.

[*The old woman locks them in.*]

Nurf. So, if you will prate, Magpies, it fhall be in a Cage. Thefe Gimcracks if they once come towards fifteen are fo gamefome, there's no riding them without a curb, nay then 'tis ten to one but that they fling the firft Adventurer out of the Saddle too. The Divel's in them I think, I'me fure in my young days. But I'de as good ftop I fhall be tempted to lie elfe. The truth is I hate all young women that are fair and there's reafon for't; if we old ones get a good look once a twelvemonth, be fure the next young one that paffes by robs us.

Enter Pacheco, Pedro, Antonio, Leandro, *and* Tutor.

Pac. Come Gentlemen, the old man's fafe, enter, and think your felves in *England*: there we run about till we find the Ladies Chambers, ranfack every thing, and are never chid except it be for not ftaying longer. What fay you, *Tutor?*

Tutor. He tells you truth Gallants, we help to drefs and undrefs faith almoft any thing; yet all the while as Vertuous as two Nuns. More, you'l find there is no other way but liberty to make us fo.

Lean. I'me glad to hear the way to Vertue is fo eafy Sir.

Ant. I alwayes thought it, there's none but a company of ill-natur'd morofe people that would have it hard can think it otherwife.

Ped. Can any one believe that fuch a glorious thing as woman is, was made to be conceal'd?

                                   Ant.

Ant. No, 'tmuſt be curſed Hereſie, I had rather they ſhould put out the Sun by half.

Pache. That's becauſe you love their company in the dark. Was not that good, *Tutor*? (*Aſide.*)

Tut. Excellent!

Sees the old Nurſe.   *Ped.* Hey day! who have we here? I have heard of Guardian Angels, but never thought that Divels were ſo employed before.

Tutor. You know the faſhion Sir of your own Country. This is the ſweet-meat keeper, the preſerver of Maiden-heads that ſhall for a Ducat corrupt youth, and teach them more bawdy in a week than half a dozen years practice; yet is truſted with as much beauty as is able to make the great *Turks* Empire run mad, merely for being old and ill natur'd. In ſhort Sir here our *Reformation* muſt begin.

Ant. Come at her then.

Nurſ. What do you mean Gentlemen? I'me onely a poor old Servant to the houſe.

Pedro. Thy being old is enough to make us hate thee.

Pacheco. Come where are my Siſters? give me the keys.

Nurſ. No ſuch matter, my Maſter charged me but juſt now to the contrary, and I will be true.

Pacheco. Give me them you Witch or----

Nurſ. I'le cry out, will you force me?

Pedro. Have you got them?   [*He takes away the keys*]

Pacheco. Yes, Yes.

Pedro. But how ſhall we ſtop her mouth? an old womans tongue is harder to lay than ten Divels.

Anto. Let me alone with her, I go always prepared to ſtop theſe noiſes.

[*Ant. Gags and binds her and throws her out*]

Ant. There lie thee there, and dare but ſo much as think miſchief, and do you hear I'le pull out the two ſtumps that are left.

Pacheco. Here Gallants take theſe keys. Now you may enter and catch who catch can *a la mode d' Angleterre*, I diſturb nobody not I.

Ant.

Ant. A kind Brother this! *(Afide)* it fhall go hard but I will have a Sifter for you Sir.   [*Exeunt* Pedro, Antonio.

(Afide) *Lea.* My jealoufie makes it but too true I am in love, and that with fuch refpect that 'tis impoffible to benefit by this freedom.

Tut. Courage Sir, I perceive you are one of the cold con-templative lovers that follow a Miftrifs at a diftance, and think your felf happy if you purchafe one gracious nod, with ten thoufand cringes.   In for fhame.

Pacheco. If you'l carry me to one of your Ladies, I'le foon teach you better courtfhip.   Or if you'l ftay here. You fhall fee me practife.

Lean. I fhall be glad to learn Sir.

Pacheco. Come *Tutor* fhow me the way of addrefs to a Lady.

Tutor. Did you never fee the Gallants in the Antechamber, how they prepare themfelves before entrance?

Pacheco. Yes I warrant, what was I in *England* fo long for elfe? but will that do?

Tutor. The very fame.   ⎡ *Sets his wig and fhirt*
Pacheco. Then thus.   ⎣ *and tricks himfelf.*

How do you like this Sir?

Lea. Oh Sir much beyond any thing I ever faw.   I muft have patience with this fool for his Sifters fake. *(Afide.)*

Tutor Then Sir we don't go your formal old way of mak-ing legs, as if we had fome Deity to worfhip.   But knowing they are flefh and blood as well as we approach briskly.

Pacheco. Begin with an oath or two.   I think it is not much matter whether it be to the purpofe or not *Tutor.*

Tutor. Not at all Sir, they'l excufe all that follows for the fake of that.

Lean. Thefe are great fecrets, you improve me Gentlemen.

Pac. Nay Sir, if we carry on our *Reformation,* the whole ftate will ftand engaged to us, but great defigns feldom prof-per at the firft.

Lean. The more's our ignorance, but pray Sir in.   If there be fuch a toy as a Mafque or Fan to play with, or you can find any thing new about her to commend 'tis modifh, and the moft gentile fubject for difcourfe.

Tut. If you name two or three Ladies of quality familiarly, it founds well and brings you in esteem. But most of all if you can learn who she hates (for women have always little quarrels amongst themselves) and can pick up a story to their disadvantage, you render your self beyond exception acceptable.

Pacheco. I do it alwayes, but nothing pleases them so much as a little sprinkling of bawdy *Tutor.* Only the Divels in't, the rogues perpetually out-do me at it.

Tutor. No wonder Sir, they practise daily, and no three women that are acquaintance but make a Bawdy language for their own use.

Pach. I wish you had a Sister Sir, or so, that you might see me practise or'e these lectures,

Lean. 'Tis my misfortune Sir.

Pache. But suppose for once that you were my Mistriss.

Lea. Content.

Pacheco. Thus I come up.   [*Sings a piece of a Tune.*]
And how ? damn me Madam all a mort ?

Tutor. Incomparably well!

Lean. Must I swear too ?

Pach. No Sir by no means, if the women once get that (as there is a faction amongst them that endeavour it) they rob us of half our discourse. But say what you will I have nevvs from the last Ball, or of some nevv Beauty kept by such a one. Or a nevv Play to find fault vvith or commend according as I hear vvho made it.

Tutor. And vvhen you once get them into the discourse of Plays they'l run on themselves. Praise such an Actor for this part, a second for another, a third for a comely man, a fourth for dancing vvell.

Pache. Nay Sir, if you meet vvith a vvoman that does not find you discourse on this subject, conclude her some Jilt that never had the good luck to be pickt up there, or some poor vvhore that can't purchase a seat.

Lean. But vvhat do you do all the time?

Pache. Comb my Wig by her glass and tvventy other
                                                    gentile

gentile tricks. But you muſt have time to learn, I my ſelf am beholden to travel, and this good man my *Tutor* here.

Lea. I deſpair of e're attaining ſuch perfections.

Pache. Induſtry may do much, Sir.

Enter Pedro, Antonio, Mariana, Iſmena.

Tutor. So, here they come; does not this look better than making legs to a belcony and blowing kiſſes up and down.

Pache. This is right. Bleſt *Reformation!*

(*Aſide*) *Lean.* I find this Engliſh cuſtom will not down with me, I'me too much an *Italian* not to be jealous of the thing I love.

Mari. You may think us rude for to be thus familiar; but a Fathers ſtrictneſs, and my Brothers good leſſons have in-ſtructed us.

Pedro. It's nothing Madam but what becomes all People that are Vertuous; 'tis only ſuch as drive a trade, and gain by ſeeming nice that ſhould be otherwiſe.

Iſm. Phy Siſter, you ſin againſt our Covenant to go about t'excuſe your ſelf; for my part I think we need none, I'me ſure our ſouls are free as any mans: And yet forſooth our bodies muſt be confin'd, and that by old men and women too, people by their very natures made unfit for liberty.

Anto. Brave Virago! You ſhall be our Captain Madam in this holy war.

Pach. She's my own Siſter Sir, you ſee that.

(of *Leandro.*) This is a modeſt Gentleman of the *Reforma-tion*, pray bid him welcome. I and my *Tutor* have been read-ing to him and we have hopes of his improvement.

Mar. Your friend muſt challenge welcome here, Brother.

Iſm. The being a Reformer gives it him in's own right.

Lean. You heap your honors too faſt on me Ladies, and the obligation is too far above my merit.

Pach. There's ſtuff indeed. Can't you ſerve her as I told you I would one of your Siſters? But the firſt fault ſhall be pardon'd.

Lean. Still worſe it gnaws here. (*Aſide.*)

Mar. Fie Brother, the Gentleman ſpeaks well.

F

Pach.

Pach. Yes if he would hold up his head a little, and not begin with such a long word as obligation.

Lean. I have loft all patience. (*Aside.*)

Pach. Mark Sir, you should cringe thus, speak two or three half sentences, as, I vow Madam, take me but, and all that. And then come up boldly.

Lean. (*Aside*) 'Tis well you are her Brother. I find I must contrive my ends some other way, And when she's once a wife she shall obey.
[*Exit* Leandro.

Tut. You may end your Lecture, the Gentleman's gone Sir.

Pach. Gone! then let him live in ignorance.

Mari. If you're always thus exact brother, we shall ne're increase our Company.

Ant. You must pardon him, he was always humorsome.

Pach. 'Tis strange, when People have such opportunities and wont improve themselves.

Enter Pisauro.

Art thou come dear Rogue? let me kiss the. Here Sisters, share him, this is my second that I told you of. If we meet with any opposition in our great affair.

Pis. But that we meet on the design of freedom Ladies, I might easily have been thought rude to have intruded thus.

If. Nothing but your free humor can make you welcome here.

Pis. 'Twould be happiness to purchase it at any rate, but this doubles the favour Madam.

Mar. Fie Sir, this founds too like a Compliment. We should be loth to lose the good opinion we have of you.

Pach. Have done for shame or I shall read you one of your friend *Leandros* Lectures.

Pis. Pray what have you done to make him leave your Company?

Ped. Trust me nothing but mirth, but Lovers are humorsome.

Pis. Sir, no more.

Pach. Come Gallants now we're met, what think you of a Dance?

Anto. We want Musick and Ladies.

Pach.

Pach. Not fo faft good Sir, here's two to four of you, in *England* 'tis common to go halfes, and the women never complain neither. No, no. The Muſick, is the thing. Oh *Tutor* for the four and twenty Englifh Violins now. You'd think your felves in Heaven, Gentlemen, at a new Play. There we ftand up with our Miftreſſes in our hands, keep time and court them to the humor of the aire, have one particular fort of ftrain to gripe at, another for a languifhing look. We *Italians* find fault with your *Tramontanes,* but we are dull we are dull to them.

Piſa. Pray let's defer that for our next meeting; if thefe Ladies will but honor me to be my gueſts, I'le take care thefe wants fhall be fupplied.

Pach. I'le engage for them.

Mar. Now we have begun this way of freedom we fhould be uncivil to deny you Sir.

Iſm. But how fhall we get looſe?

Piſa. That fhall be provided for before we part. It is but juſt the firſt time be ſpent in the publick fervice.

Tut. Some Chairs there.

Anto. Well propoſed, and that the rules of *Reformation* be decreed by joint confent.

Ped. At leaſt that every one fhould undertake befides the Generall work, fome one particular for to advance the *Reformation.*

Piſ. Let's to the confultation then.

Ped. Firſt I propoſe *Pacheco* be voted perpetual Chair-man to the Society; as one of whoſe faithfulneſs and zeale we've had fufficient proof.

All. Agreed.

Pach. W'accept the honor Gentlemen, and hope we may deferve it by our future diligence.

[*Sits down*]

Ant. Come Ladies will it pleaſe you fit.

Iſm. Do you uſe t'admit of women to your privy counſel?

Ped. Yes Madam they ftill have had the cafting vote in every *Reformation.*

Mar.

Mar. Nay then wee'l never lofe our Priviledge.

Pach. Firft I declare my *Tutor* fecretary. [*They fit down.*]

Pif. You've made a happy choice.

Pach. Next, as a thing that's very much conducing to the *Reformation,* I undertake to regulate and be the pattern of all fafhions in the town. To further which my Secretary fhall difpatch and keep a correfpondence with our beloved pattern *England.*

Pif. Why not with *France* ? they borrow all from thence.

Tut. True Sir, and I have known fome fcores of Gallants that fail thither twice or thrice a year on that defign. And are expected by the reft with as much earneftnefs as the Eaft-*India* fleet by thofe that make the greateft venture.

Pach. Yes *Tutor,* but they make fome new additions of their own; as your fring'd glove, curle of the wig, or cut of the belt, which ftrikes me ftrangely. Befides, they much improve the gate and ceremony. And out-do the *French* in their own way cringe and wadle.

Ped. Thefe are Arguments beyond objection. I under-take t'invent a Language for the company, I mean fome twenty words or more of conftant ufe. Or fenfe or not, all's one fo long as fafhionable.

Pach. Good, and the true Genteel Englifh way of wit. You fhall have a Gallant pay his devoirs, teftifie his amours, and make his affignations fome twenty times a day.

Ped. To this I'le add as many ftories too. To which we muft refer all our difcourfe. This ferves inftead of whifpering.

Tut. Oh much better ; but then the Ladies muft engage to feem to underftand and laugh at all you fay.

Mar. That's eafy, for we always do pretend to know more than we do.

Ifm. 'Tis but as all that would be thought great wits do, Sifter.

Pif. I have a project now on foot which will advance the *Reformation,* but beg I may once more try the experiment before I do reveal't.

Pach. It's granted. What fay you *Antonio?*

Ant.

Ant. Why I will undertake for to reform all the old men in *Venice* to the Englilh way. Expect within a week to fee them in their Wigs and with their chins new fhav'd, like boys of fi'tcen. Nay more, I do intend for to begin with old *Camillo* too himfelf.

Pif. 'Tis a bold project, fucceed or not.

Tut. For my part I'le ftick to my old way and write you Plays and Songs. I know they never fail. I'le undertake the laft nevv Play or tvvo I vvrit made the young Ladies more free, and brought more kind couples together, than all the old vvomen or Pages in the Country.

Pach. *Probatum eft.* I've reap'd the benefit of that my felf. What fay the Ladies novv ?

Mar. We can only promife for to follovv your inftructions, Gentlemen.

Ifm. And that vve do in every thing: vvith a little more experience we may venture to undertake fome project of our felves.

Ant. Bravely refolved Ladies. No caufe can fail that's backt by two fuch Champions.

Tut. Will you give me leave to give you fome advice.

Pach. Leave? you're *Tutor* to the Society.

Tut. Then firft ----

Mar. Heark what noife is that, for Heaven fake look out, Oh we're undone Sifter.

Ifm. 'Twill be in good company then.

Tut. 'Tis *Antonio's Boy.*

Enter Boy.

Ant. Is he coming ?

Boy. Yes Sir.

Pach. Away with thefe things there quickly.

Boy. He is not very near yet.

Ant. Go out and give us more notice.   [*Exit* Boy.

Pif. Ladies, if you follow my advice you may have freedom without fear.

Ifm. We'l follow any thing to purchafe that.

Pif. Here onely take this Powder, and when your Father

calls

calls for wine mingle it with this, within an hour it will make him ſleep, and you free.

Mar. But is there no danger Sir?

Piſ. A child may take it Madam.

Enter Boy.

Boy. He's juſt here.

Ant. Then we have no time for complement.

Piſ. You remember your promiſe Ladies. Come *Pacheco* you ſhall go along with me, it ſhall be hard but I will have a Miſtriſs for you. This does but ſet thy teeth on edge.

Pach. This way, this way, by the back door.

[*Exeunt, Omnes præter* Mar. Iſm.
[Mariana *and* Iſmena *pull out their works.*]

Mar. Pray Siſter let's be very dutiful for fear he ſhould miſtruſt.

Iſm. I warrant you; do you think I am to learn to counterfeit at fifteen?

Enter Camillo.

Cam. Now I'me pleaſed, be ſtill thus dutiful, and you ſhall find me an Indulgent Father. I am contriving ſomething unto your advantage *Mariana*, you ſhall hear it ſhortly.

Mar. I ſhall wait your commands Sir.

Cam. That was well ſaid, and for you too *Iſmena.*

Iſm. If it pleaſes you Sir I muſt needs be ſatisfied, I was always taught to be dutiful.

Cam. Thou haſt thy Mothers ſoul. I am o'rejoy'd to find thee thus. Where's the *Nurſe?*

Iſm. I forgot to tell you Sir, as ſoon as you went out, ſhe was taken with a moſt violent raving fit. And talkt and rayled ſo loud ſhe quite frighted us.

Mar. Then on the ſudden was ſtruck dumb. And has not ſpoke one word ſince.

Cam. Poor woman. I'le go ſee her.

Iſm. No, pray Sir ſhe's now faſt and you'l diſturb her.

Nurſe within makes a noiſe. *Cam.* Well thought on, 'tis only reſt that muſt compoſe her. But hark what noiſe is that! Again!

Iſm.

Ism. 'Tis the *Nurse*, for Heaven fake Sifter run and ungag (to *Mar.*) her we're undone elfe, and leave me to my Father.

[*Exit* Mari,

Cam. What's the houfe hanted at this time of day?

Ism. 'Tis only the poor *Nurfe* Sir that wakes in her diftracted fit.

Enter Nurfe *and* Mariana.

Mar. Good dear, dear *Nurfe.*

Nurfe. Not I, it fhall out.

Mar. I'le give you my beft Peticoat, good *Nurfe.*

Nurf. Not all the world fhall hire me. Oh Sir!

Ism. Pray Sifter help me to hold her. Her fit increafes, Lord how her eyes rowl! (*Afide*) Sweet *Nurfe* I'le give thee any thing.

Nur. Oh Mafter! Such a noife, fuch finging, nay pray Heaven it were no worfe, for they were roaring Boys.

Cam. She raves indeed, what doft mean *Nurfe*?

Nurfe. I mean here Sir, with your daughter fome five or fix of them.

Mar. Poor old creature, how ftrong her fancy is? let's bind her Sir, they fay that that will hinder it.

Cam. Here's no body but I and you and my two daughters.

Nurf. But there was Sir. Heaven grant you have no grand-children in ftore, for I begin to doubt them.

Ism. Juft thus fhe talkt before fhe flept, a little Opium would do well to fettle her. (good *Nurfe.* (*Afide*)

Nurfe. You think to carry it off, but now my Gag's out it fhall be known. And how you contrived.

Cam. I found them here at work alone.

Nurfe. I'me apt to think they're work was done before you came Sir.

Cam. Pray *Ifmena*, what does fhe mean by this?

Ism. Heaven knows, fome fad diftraction Sir, I doubt fhe has been wicked in her youth.

Nurf. Come, Come I doubt you are. I fee old Age and Service cannot be believed.

Ism.

Ism. Mark Sister, now she's in her crying fit too. I'le call for help and put her to bed.

Enter Servant.

Ser. Here's a Gentleman without that calls himself *Leandro*, Sir, has business with you.

Cam. I come, carry out the *Nurse* and let the Maids look after her.   [*Exit* Camillo.

Mar. I think they had best bind her. Pray Heaven she do no mischief.

Ism. Her teeth are all out, she can't bite.

Mar. Now what do you think on't *Nurse?*

Nur. I think you're all possest, for to abuse me thus. All that vexes me, I ne're deserv'd it at my Masters hands. But I will be reveng'd.   [*Exit* Nurse.

Ism. This is beyond expectation. Pray Heaven our next frolick succeed as well.

Mar. I'me strangely afraid of this *Leandro*.

Ism. That's the Melancholy man that was with us, is it not?

Mar. The same; if he betray us we're undone yet.

Ism. Ne're fear wench, this powder will be one shift more.
 And whether Fortune smiles or knits her brow,
We can't be worse than slaves, and so we're now.
                      [*Exeunt* Ism. Mari.

Enter Camillo, Leandro.

Lean. I thought my self engaged besides the particular love I bear your daughter, by my tie to honor to declare this truth.

Cam. 'Tis very strange.

Lean. The *Nurse* can justifie it.

Cam. Why, she's distracted Sir.

Lean. She might well seem so, abused as she has been.

Cam. Come in with me and wee'l examine further, and if it does prove true, I stand obliged.

Lean. If not, then take your own revenge.

                      [*Exeunt.*

Juliana, Lelia.

Jul. 'Twas well we had this notice, we had been surprized else. What unlucky business brings him back? Now must I be
                                        kist

kift and hugg'd by one I hate. Phaugh. He faid *Lyfander* told it him himfelf, did he not?

Lel. Yes, Madam.

Jul. Very well, the more he doats on's Mis, the more time fhall I have with my Gallant, and if he does chance to find me out I have fomething to cry quit with. In the mean time I'le feem as fond as ever, left he fhould fufpect me.

Lel. Heark Madam, I think I hear him coming.

Jul. Yes, 'tis he.

Enter Lyfander.

Next I will have you work the difmal ftory of poor *Ari-adnes* love, and how the cruel *Thefeus* left her, 'twas unkindly done *Lelia* : But men are not fo fond as we.

Lyf. Pox of your counterfeit pipe, he has been here but fled. *(Afide.)*

Jul. Ar't' come deareft? now thou'rt kind indeed, a fud-dain joy o'rewhelming me. I was juft talking of the cruelties of men, and pittying our poor fex. But I had never yet a caufe to doubt of thee. Ten thoufand welcomes. I have had fuch fears.

Lyf. Left I fhould come home too foon *(Afide.)* Thou art fo fond, I muft believe thee, I am o'rejoy'd to find thee in this health. Truft me I've fcarcely flept fince laft we parted.

Jul. No, you had one that kept you waking *(Afide)* Poor Dear I pitty thee; you wanted me to fing and kifs thee to thy reft.

Lyf. Truth is, no Opium caufes fleep fo much as fuch a bed-fellovv. ----I hate *(Afide.)*

Jul. Nay I my felf have had the ftrangeft dreams too.

Lyf. I hope they vvere all pleafant ones.

Jul. They vvere all of you, you night and day difpofe my thoug'ts. One time methoughts you loved another vvoman more than me, that troubled me a little, as it vvould any vvife that loves fo vvell as I do. But I believe there are but fevv.

Lyf. Heaven forbid there fhould. *(Afide)* That vvas thy

too

too much fondne(s, thou can'ft not have thofe thoughts avvake.

Jul. No deareft joy, 'tvvas only in a dream.

Lyf. That's nothing, for I had fuch a one of you, but when I wak'd I chid my felf.

Jul. Nay, then we're even, and muft pardon one another.

Lel. There's reafon for't, for you are both finners. *(Afide.)*

Lyf. I am fo far from a miftruft, that I dare fwear thou art as innocent, as I my felf.

Jul. I dare pawn my innocence for thee too.

Lel. And if you ne're redeem't 'tis no great lofs. *(Afide.)*

Jul. But why fhould we talk thus ? it looks too like miftruft. Believe me t'was with me an Age till your return.

Lyf. The very laft hour before mine, feemed months to me too. I would fain have taken you napping. *(Afide.)*

Jul. Poor rogue, you're thin fince laft I faw you, you fhall not go agen.

Lelia. A Miftrifs and a Wife's enough to mak any body look fo. *(Afide.)*

Lyf. Nay deareft but I muft, and leave thee for a week or two, an hour is the longeft of my ftay.

Jul. And of my life. You will kill me.

Lyf. It fhall be with kindnefs then.

Jul. A week ! I know thou'rt not in earneft but vvilt deceive me thus agen, come prithee do, thefe furprizes make thy coming ten times pleafanter.

Lel. That vvas vvell nickt, to make fure vvork. *(Afide.)*

Lyf. 'Tis too certain, *Juliana*, that's the leaft; nay, never cry for't. But let's enjoy that little time vve have, come prithee leave.

They fay that married peoples Loves decay,

But mine ftill grovvs.

Jul. And mine, ----another vvay. *(Afide.)*

A C T

ACT IV. SCENE I.

Pisauro, Antonio, Pedro.

Pis. COme bang't, vvhy all this mincing? can you imagine I'me fo dull as not to fee through it? Ten to one I knovv the caufe of your Mumps; as much, I find the rife of your fullennefs. In fhort *Pedro* you have a months mind to meafure lengths vvith Madam *Mariana,* and you *Antonio* have as much to a day to try hovv things vvill fit vvith brisk *Ifmena.* Come, confefs, confefs; I fee plainly by your folemn pace and grave contriving looks, you have been running over all the ftories in Romances to accomplifh your defigns.

Ped. I muft declare that I have no averfion to the freedom of her humour.

Ant. And I have feen fome faces and conditions which I have liked much worfe. But----

Pis. Pox on you both! don't you think this founds very prettily to one that has been an Adventurer, in this trade of love? You muft give me leave to know that your no averfion is the height of defire, and your liking much worfe is the fame with nothing half fo well. But this filly love ftill thinks, becaufe he's blind himfelf, no body elfe muft fee.

Ped. Nay, Pray *Pifauro,* for charity invent fome other name, though it fhould prove the felf fame thing, for this is fcandalous.

Ant. No, No, 'tis fo, I plainly fee all men have a certain time allowed to play the fool, and love in, and this is mine.

Pis. This is honeft and a friendly part. But why the Divel don't you tell them fo? you fee we're more put to't to lay the jealoufie of old *Camillo,* than we fhould be to raife a Ghoft, to gain an houres leifure.

Ant. I thought I ventured fair confidering t'was the firft time.

Pis.

Pif. That's very fine, the firſt time? is not the Gallant worthy more applauſe that hits the mark, the firſt ſhoot, than he that draws a dozen times and ne're comes nigh the ſpot? I'me ſure the Ladies will commend him for his aime.

Ped. But you know the Cuſtom does require Ceremony.

Pif. As for cuſtomes, our *Reformation* is deſign'd for to deſtroy them all. And this firſt in ſhort Gentlemen, there are but two wayes you can deſign to be poſſeſſours of your hopes: either to perſwade them to their faſhionable way of love, or be content your ſelves to marry them.

Ant. But neither of theſe, I doubt, will do, *Piſauro*; 'tis certain they are too wiſe and vertuous for the firſt; too briſk and jolly for the ſecond.

Pif. Truth is, their briſkneſs makes me fear they are honeſt.

Ped. Could I find them otherwiſe, I ſhould ſoon make an end of all my love.

Ant. Faith, thought I formerly have had no great opinion of the other, yet I reſolve to try it now, and carry on the *Reformation* too. *Venice* ſhall learn from me the freedom due to Wives. What ſayeſt thou, *Pedro*?

Ped. Nay, I am too much thy friend to leave thee in the greateſt hazard of thy life.

Pif. Well agreed. I ſhall give you opportunity anon, if my deſign ſucceeds with old *Camillo*: though I begin to doubt becauſe the *Tutor* comes not. By this *Pacheco* and his Miſtriſs have chang'd a broad-ſide or two; I left them nigh engaging.

Ped. There is no danger in the combat I preſume.

Pif. Faith, not on her ſide, ſhe has little to loſe beſides the Veſſel, let him board her when he will.

Ant. Have you got the *Tutors* conſent yet?

Pif. That I intend to buy with gold and good words, and the money will be well put out to uſe too; the fool muſt needs be rich, and the wench I know has wit enough to wheadle him.

Ped. But do you think he'le bite home enough to marry?

Pif. Yes, I know ſhe'l ſtand upon her honour, the un-

known

known value of a womans credit, and twenty such common places they all inherit from their Mothers, and if he once grow hot he will do any thing.

Ant. Have you heard any news of *Leandro*?

Pif. Yes, but am loth to tell a story so imperfect; the *Tutor* will tell us all.

Ped. Does that Fellow continue his old humour still?

Pif. Without the least change, if not improved.

Ant. Prithee put him into 't a little.

Pif. You'l repent you, for 'tis intolerable.

Ped. No, No, for once we'l venture it.

Ant. 'Tis much that this fellow that has wit, and is company in every thing besides, should thus besot himself.

Ped. Let's work a cure and beat him out of this humour.

Pif. If beating would have done he had been well long ere this.

Ant. Methinks change of air should work.

Pif. No, nothing, he picks out half a dozen young fools where e're he comes, sticks to them till he has talk'd o're all he has to say, and then changes. But st.

Enter Tutor.

Here he comes, let's dispatch our business first: Welcome Sir, what news? you look as if you'd had a Play hist, or met with some presumptuous fool that would pretend to understand the rules of Poetry in your company.

Tut. No none of these, but something that concerns you nearer at the present: in short, *Leandro* has betray'd all, renounced his covenant, and become Reprobate.

Ant. Faith, I expected no better, I knew he must necessarily turn Heretick by this way of living: alas, he drunk nothing but *Penitential* water and dangerous Coffee, half a dozen such Sneaks would ruin the Republick.

Ped. Prithee, what new light or Revelation rules him now?

Tut. The old flame of Love, and he goes the old *Italian* way to work too: makes his addresses to the Father without consulting the woman: Has told of your being there, the Rules of your *Reformation*; and by this art so wheadled
him

'him that he refolves to marry one of his daughters to him immediately; to which end he's juft now gone to fetch a Prieft. Yonder has been fuch a Lecture, what between the old man and the *Nurfe*, that the Poor Ladies have been worried.

Ant. Which of the Sifters is't?

Pif. *Ifmena*, that's it which vexes me, h'as pickt the flower out of all our conqueft.

Ant. But he fhall hang before he e're fhall wear her.

Ped. No, it muft not be; if we let the firft rebellion profper, we betray the weaknefs of our Government.

Pif. I knew him falfe before, and therefore promifed to affift you in your loves, from hence I do renounce all friendfhip with him as a Traytor.

Ant. Thou art truly Loyal. Pray let me beg the freedom to contrive his punifhment; if I make him not as wretched and ridiculous as his worft of enemies can wifh, truft me with no more affairs of State.

Ped. But how fhall we efcape this danger?

Pif. Has he taken the powder yet?

Tut. Yes, that's all our hopes. He railed himfelf fo dry that he was forced to call for wine. If that works before *Leandro* comes, we fhould be freed for the prefent, the *Nurfe* too has a dofe to fpoil her talking.

Ant. That's well, could we but meet him.

Tut. He muft come this way, for he went towards the Arfenal.

Ant. Then we are fafe, let me alone to manage him.

Pif. In the mean time let us divert our felves.

Tut. I thought to have met *Pacheco* here, 'tis certain he muft not come nigh home till old *Camillo* is appeafed; nor I neither.

Pif. He's in a fafer place practifing all his Lectures over to his Miftrifs. I have a project now on foot which if you'l promife to advance you fhall want no gold; but of that anon.

Tut. I fhall endeavour to ferve you Sir.

Pif. Come Sir you are a judge, what opinion have you of the laft new Play?

Tut.

Tut. Faith---- well for an essay. I guess the Gentlemans but a beginner. I my self----

Pif. Now he's in. *(Aside.)*

Tut. Writ with the same much success at first, 'twas industry and much converse that made me ripe; I tell you Gentlemen, when I first attempted this way I understood no more of Poetry than one of you.

Ped. This is strange impudence. ⎱
Ant. 'Tis nothing yet.   ⎰ *Aside.*

Tut. There are many pretenders but you see how few succeed; and bating two or three of this nation as *Tasso*, *Ariosto* and *Guarini*, that write indifferently well, the rest must not be named for Poesy: we have some three or four, as *Fletcher*, *Iohnson*, *Shakespear*, *Davenant*, that have scribled themselves into the bulk of follies and are admired to, but ne're knew the laws of heroick or dramatick poesy, nor faith to write true English neither.

Ant. 'Tis very much, I hope Sir your heroick play goes on.

Tut. As fast as a piece of that exactness can. I'le only leave a pattern to the world for the succeeding ages and have done.

Ped. Oh Sir you'l wrong the world.

Tut. No faith Sir I grow weary of applause.

Ant. Will you give me leave to ask the way for others to attain to your perfection?

Tut. I will not say but that it may be done, but trust me you'l find it hard Gentlemen, and since you are my friends I'le tell you.

Ped. You will oblige us Sir.

Tut. First I speak of Tragedy, which let the world say what it will and doat on little things, I scrible now and then, as good faith they doe Gentlemen strangely; you shall have them---- but I don't love to praise my self. Tragedy I say's my Masterpiece.

Ant. Every tthing you do seems so.

Tut. Nay, nay, pray forbear Gentlemen----To go on: I take a subject, as suppose the Siege of *Candy*, or the conquest

of

of *Flanders*, and by the way Sir let it alwayes be some war-like action; you can't imagine what a grace a Drum and Trumpet give a Play. Then Sir I take you some three or four or half a dozen Kings, but most commonly two or three serve my turn, not a farthing matter whether they lived within a hundred years of one another, not a farthing Gentlemen, I have tryed it, and let the Play be what it will, the Characters are still the same.

Pif. Trust me Sir, this is a secret of your art.

Tut. As Sir you must alwayes have two Ladies in Love with one man, or two men in love with one woman; if you make them the Father and the Son, or two Brothers, or two Friends, 'twill do the better. There you know is opportunity for love and honour and Fighting, and all that.

Ped. Very well Sir.

Tut. Then Sir you must have a Hero that shall fight with all the world; yes i'gad, and beat them too, and half the gods into the bargain if occasion serves.

Ant. This method must needs take.

Tut. And does Sir. But give me leave and mark it for infallible, in all you write reflect upon religion and the Clergy; you can't imagine how it tickles, you shall have the Gallants get those verses all by heart, and fill their letters with them to their Country friends; believe me this one piece of art has set off many an indifferent Play, and but you are my friends----

Ant. You honour us.

Tut. Last of all, be sure to raise a dancing singing ghost or two, court the Players for half a dozen new scenes and fine cloaths (for take me if there ben't much in that too) put your story into rime, and kill enough at the end of the Play, and *Probatum est* your business is done for Tragedy.

Pif. A'n't you weary?

Ped. No prithee let him run on. } *side.*

Tut. Then as for Comedy, which I was saying my Genius does not lead me to, but that the world may know I can at idle houres when I please out-write them, I do venture at.

Pif.

Pif. And with fuccefs Sir too, believe it.

Tw. And faith Gentlemen I'le tell you, there's your *French* Nation, Pox on't a kind of Jack-pudding wit, yet hang me if their Plays be well pick'd, as a fcene here and a fcene there, it will do it, it will i' faith, I have try'd it.

Ped. Well Sir proceed.

Tw. But your true Englifh and my way, is to write your Plays with double fence and brisk meaning Songs. Take me, you fhall have the Ladies laugh at a little bawdy jeft as if they would bepifs themfelves, and the young Mounfieurs clap as if they meant to wear their hands out in the fervice: and if you confider, this is eafy and a large fubject, efpecially to one that will be at the charge to keep a wench that underftands her trade, you can't imagine what hints and pretty things fhe will pick up. Now Sir, if you can but maintain two or three of thofe Characters, no matter what your plot is, your love and honour will do here agen, and 'tis but faving alive and marrying thofe that you would kill in Tragedy, and you have done.

Ant. We give you thanks for thefe inftructions, and fhall endeavour to improve Sir.

Tw. Nay, I have not done yet, but if you promife fecrecy will let you know my great Arcanum.

All. We do.

Tw. 'Tis this, when I have writ a Play, I pick fome Lady out of general acquaintance, or favourite at the Court, that would be thought a wit, and fend it in pretence for to fubmit it to her judgment. This fhe takes for fuch a favour--- and raifes her efteem fo much--fhe talks of nothing elfe but Mr. fuch a ones new Play, and picks out the beft on't to repeat, fo half the town by this means is engag'd to clap before they come.

Ped. Excellent!

Tw. Befides this, I take fome half a dozen youngfters of the town, People that pride themfelves in one of my nods or a fhaking by the hand at the Coffee-houfe, and let them have a copy of a Song or two, or promife of the Prologue, which does fo much oblige, that I have all the faction of the town that makes a noife on my fide.

H   *Ant.*

Ant: Truſt me Sir theſe are very great rules.

Tut. And ſuch as never fail, but I am reſolv'd to leave, and having made a pattern for the world ſo long deceiv'd in their opinion of wit and Language.

Ped. For heaven ſake pitty us now *Piſauro,* and perſwade him to keep this for his *(Aſide)* Preface to the next new Play.

Piſ. Not I, ſince you have wound him up, may you be deaf with noiſe.

Ant. Here comes one that will releaſe us then.

Enter Leandro.

Piſ. We muſt keep him in talk a while. *(Aſide.)*

Leandro here ! that's a miracle, where haſt thou been for heavens ſake? thou might'ſt have found the North paſſage to the *Indies* ſince I ſaw thee.

Lean. Troth Gentlemen I have found out as difficult a one to as pleaſant a place, and am juſt going to reap the benefit of my adventure.

Ant: We may all ſhare I hope.

Lea. No, I'me forc'd to monopoliſe for all the ſweets and treaſures of the place, if once they're blow'd upon or toucht by more than one, loſe all their value and delight.

Ped. Are you the firſt diſcoverer that you challenge ſuch propriety?

Lea. I've reaſon to think ſo, for th' acceſſes were all guarded by a watchful dragon.

Ant. In plain language Sir.

Lea. I'le tell you then becauſe I am in haſt; ſince I left you I have been with old *Camillo,* drawn up writings, agreed every thing between us, and only want a Prieſt (which is juſt going thither) to make *Iſmena* mine; was not my paſſage ſhorter than ordinary, Gentlemen, and the Iſland worth diſcovery? Pray Gentlemen how does the *Reformation* go forward?

Piſ. But haſt thou no remorſe, no pricking all this time?

Lean. For what prithee?

Piſ. Is thy zeal for the ſolemn covenant ſo ſoon forgot? how dares thou ſin after this rate and rob a woman of her
liberty

liberty which thou haſt ſworn to defend at leaſt, if not procure?

Ped. You are too haſty *Piſauro,* without queſtion he will give her all ſhe wiſhes and the *Reformation* askes.

Lean. No, you're deceiv'd Sir, though I was Engliſh when a batchelour, I'le be a true *Italian* and my ſelf, when married. I value her credit and my quiet too much to do otherwiſe.

Piſ. Then may all *Cupids* curſes light upon thee.

Lean. I dare venture ten times more than that blind boy is able to inflict for ſuch a prize, farewel Gentlemen.

Ant. Nay, ſtay and take all with you, may'ſt thou be impotent in th' height of all thy wiſhes.

Ped. Be jealous, yet never have a cauſe.

Piſ. Run mad with dotage and ſhe ſcorn thee.

Lean. Leave, leave I ſhall grow fat with curſing.

Piſ. Thou ſhalt have enough to burſt thee then.

Ant. May'ſt thou have Sons, yet never dare to own them, and they beg their bread.

Ped. May thy daughters be ſo rank to doat on Monkeys.

Piſ. May'ſt thou live to ſee all this and hang thy ſelf. (*Laughs*) *Lean.* I'm pleas'd to ſee you envy me; and you have cauſe, for I ſhall have delights lawful and wholeſome too, when I ſhall meet you trayling of your legs after you or walking upon crutches with but one noſe among you. Adieu (*laughs*) or will you go with me and believe your eyes?

Ant. We will, lead us; and if fair means don't, force ſhall. (*Aſide.*)

[*Exeunt* Ant. Ped. Lean.

Piſ. Come *Tutor,* as we go I'le tell you my deſign which you muſt further. [*Exeunt.*

Enter Camillo, Mariana, Iſmena, Nurſe.

Cam. Come 'tis in vain to whine, I will not ſleep till I have don't.

Iſm. You may be deceiv'd for all this yet. (*Aſide.*)
Courage Siſter he begins to yawn already.

Cam. I'le ſee whether a Nunnery and a husband can re

H 2 claim

claim you. Nor fhall it go much better with your gewgaw Brother. Are you fo rampant, you muft make a decoy of my own houfe to catch your wild fowl in?

Ma. Give me fome little time for to prepare my felf.

Ca. Oh you have done that to the purpofe, finner enough to fpend the reft of your life in penitence. *(yawns.)*

Ifm. There's another, it will do. *(Afide.)*
Pray Sir let me live there and bear her company.

Cam. No, though you're both naught, I'de willingly keep one of you to breed on, and it fhall be you, a Nunnery will give you too much liberty.

If. If I muft marry give me leave to chofe.

Ca. Your choice is likely to be good by the company you keep; but I've provided for you, you fhall be kept fo clofe you fcarcely fhall have light enough *(yawns)* to read your prayers by.

If. That's too cruel, I would pray for you.

Ca. It muft be backward then; thy youth is all the reafon I can give to think thou'rt not a witch; O' my confcience thou can'ft fly, but I'le have your wings clipt, and you put into a Cage for better fecurity.

Nur. They have been wild indeed *(yawns)* took I what care I could. *(yawns.)*

Cam. Why do'ft thou yawn fo, thou infects me too. *(yawns.)*

Nur. You fee Ladies though I have no teeth I can find my tongue.

If. I prophefie that you will lofe it yet e're long, for wronging of the innocent. *[They both yawn.]*

       Enter Leandro, Anto. Pedro, Pifauro.

Cam. Welcome Son, I was waiting for you.

Lean. I've brought my friends along, the Gallants of the *Reformation*, to fee me happy and to take their leave.

Cam. I fhall take care to reform my daughters from keeping them company, *(yawns)* you have fpoiled a Son of mine too among you

Ant. Who do you fpeak Sir to?

Cam. To you all. *(yawns.)*

Nur.

Nur. To you Sir, since you are so brisk *(yawns)* this is the very Royster that gag'd and bound me Sir. *(yawns.)*

Pis. Let's look, thou gap'st as if thou had'st a gag there yet.

Lean. How is't Sir, you look not well; your eyes are heavy too.

Cam. Only a little weary and faint *(yawns)* with chiding of these wicked girles.

Lean. Wil't please you sit? A Chair there. *(Sits down.)*

Nur. How is't Sir? *(yawns.)*

Cam. Pray take away this gaping woman *(yawns)* and let us fin----fin----fin----ish---- *(Sleeps.)*

Nurs. Wil't please you to have a little *(yawns)* cordial water, or *(yawns)* some aqua mi--mirabilis, or--or.

[*Falls asleep leaning on* Cam.

(To *Ism.*) *Lean.* Believe me Madam, it proceeded all from Love.

Ism. I must obey Sir.

Pis. He's fast, he's fast Madam.

Ism. Then I am free.

Ma. And I shall scarcely say my Prayers in a Nunnery to day; how lovingly they sleep!

Lean. How's this! you have not murdered him.

Ant. Nothing but a gentle sleep Sir, which does our business as well.

Ped. Was you so ignorant to think wee'd let thee carry it thus?

Pis. What my wife Coffee-drinker over-reacht?

Lean. This is beyond all sufferance, what say you Madam? will you refuse me too?

Ism. Oh Sir, I would not marry without my Fathers leave for all the world.

Ant. Send you joy Sir, we believe our own eyes.

Lean. I'le never stay for to be baited thus.

Ant. Nay, prethee stay a while, and let me tell you a secret; you'l want news else. We gave this sleeping portion to *Camillo* and the *Nurse*, to gain an opportunity of going

out

out to laugh and dance : Remember Sir: and kept you in difcourfe till this time, when we were fure it would work, for
to prevent your marriage : Do you mark Sir ? fome few houres
hence he wakes, and then you may come again and tell your
ftory.

Lea. Yes, and be revenged.

Pif. If you dare make a fecond triall, this is but purgatory,
you know the next punifhment.

Lean. Sunk in the height of all my hopes.

[*Exit* Leandro.

Pif. Well Gallants, I'le before and leave you to wait upon the Ladies.

Ant. But whither prithee ?

Pif. To *Lyfandro*'s here hard by.

Ped. He's not at home.

Pif. But his wife is, that's as good.

Ant. Nay 'tis much better; does your furnace ftand there?

Pif. Ladies I fhall wait you.   [*Exit.*

Ma. Whofe within there ?

                              Enter Tutor.

Pray *Tutor* call fome body to carry thefe in and fet them
warm.

              Enter Servants, *carry off* Cam. Nurfe.

Ant. Now have I a ftrange defign comes into my head.

Ped. What is't?

Ant. You know Gallants I promifed to reform the old
men; what if we fhould fhave *Camillo*, head and chin, and
let him wake in a great white wig?

Ifm. For heavens fake, that would make him irreconcilea-
ble.

Ped. No, No, that's driving on too faft, we're pretty well
advanced.

Ant. I only do propofe. Come Ladies fhall we go ?

Mar. Yes Sir, I wifh our mirth ends well.

If. Fie Sifter to think of that before it does begin.

                                                      [*Exeunt.*

              Enter Pacheco, Lelia.

                                                      Pa.

Pa. I vow to gad Madam nothing but an affair of this moment and that----

Lel. Oh Sir you have honoured me.

Pa. Oh Gad Madam the honour----and but that I know your goodnels Dear Madam----let me perish but----one minute returns me as much your humble Servant, as----your Servant Madam, your fervant.

[*Exit* Pacheco.

Scena Secunda.

[Juliana *and* Lelia *laughing.*]

Jul. I'me glad to find your new gallant tickles fo.

Lel. He would make a Nun laugh that's juft profeft, and that's the forrowful'ft (*laughs*) time I can think of; all I wonder at is, that I live.

Jul. What's the matter? did he ftand upon his head or conjure, that he's fuch a miracle?

Lel. I know not what you mean by conjuring, but all the juglers at a Carnival have not fo many tricks. (*laughs.*)

Jul. I muft get fome mufick for thee, O' my confcience thou art ftung wench, prithee leave and fpeak.

Lel. Why Madam all the Painters fince the art was found out, ne're drew half the poftures he was in, in lefs than half an hour, he goes as puppets do by wiers. Pray Madam have a little patience and I'le fhew you. After a fhrug and a falute, which he tells me is the new mode, he gives his little whalebone a twirle or two.

Jul. Well then I make my curtfy.

Lel. Right Madam, then the Divel refufe him. But mine's the pleafant'ft feat in *Venice*, and that gives him opportunity to take as ftrut or two to view the room; but all this time the wig and fhirt is order'd, and as foon as e're the looking glafs was fpied, out comes the comb, and I had twenty tunes begun and never ended, or ended and ne're begun.

Jul. But what muft I do all this while?

Lel.

Lel. Admire Madam, then the posture's alter'd, and off goes the glove vvhich fhovvs the diamond ring, and out comes the gold Watch, vvhich muft be placed vvith art, for fear the chain hang not out enough to be feen.

Jul. Thou'rt a Divel to abufe him thus.

Lel. Next he approaches and knovvs I am a vvit by the chofing of my ribbons, and rails at the poor Country Madam, for making him fvveat in Summer vvith her hot colours. Next fubject of difcourfe vvas the alteration of the mode in Laces; commends my vvork, and calls all the ftitches by their proper names, and in the midft of this begins a nevv tune, fvvears 'tis good, and from thence takes occafion to run over all the Plays and his acquaintance vvith the Poets.

Jul. Could'ft thou defire better company?

Lel. Nay he has not done yet Madam; then he talks o're all the women of the town, and how *Tom* fuch a one, had turn'd off *Betty,* and *Dick* fuch another kept *Mall,* and call'd them all by their names as freely as if he had been Pimp to all the company.

Jul. And ten to one their names is all he knows them by, but you muft know 'tis modifh and a great attainment.

Lel. At laft when he came into the difcourfe of travel, I concluded vve fhould ne're have done, but all o'th' fuddain he makes me three or four cringes of feveral fafhions, begs leave for to difpatch fome great affair (which I fuppofe was to look upon fome new vvig he had befpoke) and hee'd be here immediatly.

Jul. And vvhat doft thou think of him after all this?

Lel. You muft needs guefs Madam, as of a moft egregious Fop. I'm beholden to *Pifauro* for his good vviflies.

Enter Pifauro.

And here he comes in time for to receive my thanks.

Jul. I am afhamed to hear thee talk thus, vvhat bleffing can'ft thou imagine greater than a husband that's a fool and rich?

Lel Heaven forbid Madam.

Jul. Thou'rt an Idiot: Is't not better to have him bufy himfelf himſelf with points and ribbons, toys and laces, than to be alwayes grave and melancholy, which in a while will make him jealous too and mark your very looks.

Piſ. 'Tis odds but that you're lock't up, and ſee the Sun but once a twelvemonth, and have no other company but ſome old woman that does the office of a deaths head and puts you in mind of dying.

Jul. You ſee what arts I'me forc'd to uſe to cheat *Lyſander* with, ſuch a man as this will manage all your purpoſe himſelf.

Lel. I will be rul'd by you Madam.

Piſ. 'Twas well ſaid, how did he behave himſelf?

Jul. I have had that at full, no more now I beſeech you.

Piſ. How did you carry it?

Lel. I took your directions, and had as many modiſh poſtures as I then could think on, ſometimes thus, then thus.

Piſ. That muſt needs take him, ⎰*She acts ſeveral ridicu-* did he ſpeak any thing of Love? ⎱ *lous conceited poſtures.*

Lel. I can't tell how to anſwer you, or what his way of courtſhip is when he's in earneſt, but he commended me as if I was to ſell, grip'd my hand and kiſt it, talk't of the power of love and women, and all the time ſcrew'd up and down as if he had been netled.

Piſ. Theſe are good ſigns, I ſhall know all as ſoon as e're

Pacheco ſings within. I ſee him: heark! I believe he's coming, yes 'tis he I hear him ſing, pray withdraw; the Ladies will be here immediately.

[*Exeunt* Jul. Lelia.

Enter Pacheco.

Piſ. Save you Sir, you're got off alive I ſee.

Pa. Yes faith, and that's all; hang me *Piſauro* if ſhe is not the firſt woman that has moved me on this ſide *England.*

Piſ. I thought 'twas ſhe muſt nick your humor.

Pa. Take me if ſhe has not wit too and demean, underſtands addreſs and all that.

Piſ. This character from you will raiſe her in my eſteem.

I   *Pa.*

Pa. You muſt give me leave to underſtand a little.

Piſ. You are the only judge, Sir.

Pa. Believe me ſhe has the true Court air, takes every thing that's nevv and modiſh. I'le ſvvear to you, I have ſometimes caſt an afternoon avvay, run through all my common places of diſcourſe, and at the laſt been thought ridiculous.

Piſ. You muſt meet vvith women that have been barbarous then.

Pa. No Sir, 'twas want of breeding and converſe, not one in ten that has the leaſt of it. Alas Sir, there's a particular mine, languiſhing look, and *je ne ſcay quoy*, as we ſay, and all this ſhe has in perfection. Take me, if I don't think there is a perfect ſympathy between us. But this thing of friends.

Piſ. You are Melancholy of the ſuddain.

Pa. No Sir, I am only contriving ſomething to advance our *Reformation,* and to make us perfect.

Piſ. It will do. (*Aſide.*)

Pa. And it ſhall be hard but I'le out-do you all.

Enter Anto. Pedro, Tutor, Juliana, Mariana, Iſmena, Lelia.

Jul. All the entertainment I can promiſe is your freedom, Gallants, and that you're in a houſe where you have all things at command.

Ant. There's nothing can be added Madam.

Piſ. Now you honour me, I have invited you to an Engliſh treat, Ladies, room and muſick, you bring the mirth and company with you

Some Chairs there. 　　　　　　　　　[*Chairs ſet out.*]

Pa. I have been ſo rude as to encreaſe your company without your knowledge, Sir, to day I ſvvore a ſtranger and invited him, he promiſed me to bring his Miſtriſs too.

Piſ. The leaſt acquaintance Sir with you muſt challenge welcome.

Pa. I know you'l like his humor, 'tis free beyond any thing I ever met on this ſide the *Alpes.* I in a moment found that we were made for one another's company.

Jul. That free humor which you ſpeak of brings a welcome with it.

　　　　　　　　　　　　　　　　　　　　　　　　Ped.

Ped. This looks well, we were made for this.

Ism. Methinks we begin to live now, we did but dream away our time before, Sister.

Ma. It was not half so pleasant; but now you speak of dreaming, Heaven keep my Father fast.

Ism. I resolve to think of nothing here but mirth.

Pis. Bravely said Madam. Come let's be frolick then.

Pa. My *Tutor* has provided us a dance was made to set off his new last Play in *England.*

Ant. Pray let us have it then, 'tmust be as proper here as there.

Tut. I'le step out and get it ready.

Pis. Will it please you sit Ladies? Some wine there.
[*They go to set two women together.*]

Pac. Two women together! let us never begin our *Reformation* with such a sin, come I'le teach you better, and as Master will begin an English health. Here, here stand a Lady and a Gallant. Now Madam a health to my Mis and your Gallant.

Eel. Here Sir, here's a health to my Gallant and your Mis.

Ant. Right, Right, fill it about.

Pac. So now all hands.

> *Fill round the healths good natur'd and free,*
> *Let your States-men politick be,*
> *No custom our joyes shall defer.*
> *This is bliss.*
> *Each Lady has her Gallant, each man has his Mis,*
> *On this side and this,*
> *Let us kiss, let us kiss,* A la mode d'Angle terre.

Jul. If this be an English custom, 'tis a mighty kissing country, this is too much.

Ant. Right! I knew she that liked it best would be the first that should complain. (*Aside.*)
[*They all sit a man and a woman.*]
Enter Tutor.

Tut. Strike up there.
[*Dance of Anticks.*]

Pis.

Pif. Come Sir hāve you never another health?

Pa. A thousand.

[*As he's going to drink, Enter* Lysander, Emilia.]

Lyf. Shall I keep my resolution?⎫ *Aside.*
Em. Yes prithee do for my sake.⎭

Pa. Dear heart! I wish autority can bid you welcome now.

Lyf. I thank you Sir, but I can make my self so.

Pif. 'Slife thou hast undone us man, why this is husband to the Lady in whose house we are. [*To Pac.*]

Pa. What then he's sworn, and 'tis as common for a wife to make a ball without her husbands knowledge, as for a Nun to say her Prayers; is't not *Tutor?*

Tut. Yes Sir, 'tis nothing, or with their konwledge either:

Lysander all this time compliments the Ladies. More, the good man rather than his wife shall lose a kiss, takes her by the hand and tells the next man that comes, my wife Sir, and then she's slaver'd round the company.

Ant. This must be *Lysander,* what can this come to?

Ped. At the worst we must resolve to carry off the Ladies safe.

Lyf. 'Twas kindly done to comfort up the widdow Gentlemen, come ne're disturb your selves, I'm a sworn Brother.

Pif. Resolve to carry't off briskly, there's no other way left. [*To* Juliana].

Jul. Art' come dearest? ten thousand vvelcomes, you ee vvhat shift I'm forc'd to make to comfort me in solitude; but all's too little for to make amends for one *Lysander.*

Lyf. Dear rogue thou can'st not think hovv much I vvanted thee too, you see vvhat paultry shift I vvas forced to make.

[*Shovvs Emilia.*]

Pa. She's vvondrous fair, Madam.--- [*Goes toward her.*]

Lyf. Hold, hold, Sir, though I allovv all freedom with my vvife, you knovv the English fashion is to keep my Mistris to my self.

Pa. I beg your pardon Sir, 'tvvas vvell remembred.

Jul. I see you're angry, but I vvas forced to seek to ease my grief by any vv y vvhen you vvas absent.

Lyf. Not I, ne're trouble your self to make this excuse, I
love

love this mirth ; but prithee chuck tell me, vvhich of thefe is thy Gallant ? or do they take't by turns, come prithee do, good faith I count my felf beholden to him, he eafes me.

(weeps) *Jul.* I fee no faithfulnefs can e're oblige you.

Lyf. Novv thou art too modeft, for fhame *Pifauro* ovvn her, I knovv I pay for all that finery. [*Jul. weeps.*]

Lyf. Nay vve'l be man and vvife ftill in any place but bed, and that vvant you have provided for your felf, ne're trouble your felf. If you do more than e're I could *Pifauro,* and fhe prove fruitful, I promife here to be a Godfather. If I have the fame fuccefs here, I expect the like kindnefs from you *Juliana.*

Tut. This is true love.

Pa. Novv our *Reformation* goes forvvard in good earneft.

Ma. It amazes me ; vvould I vvere free from hence once.

Lyf. Come, come, Gentlemen, be frolick, you feem rroubled ; Is not this better than flitting of nofes or a ftab Gentlemen? we can call chuck and joy and twenty fuch pretty names ftill, as well as the very beft of them.

Na, faith Ladies one dance more   [*They offer to go out.*] for my fake, I fhall grieve that I difturbed you elfe.

Mufick there (*Dance.*)

Lyf. Now be but pleas'd to take a fmall collation in the next room, and I fhall believe you think your felves welcome.

Ant. We'l wait you Sir.

Ma. Yet I'me impatient till I'me gone.

Ped. There's no danger Madam.

Ifm. I fear none Sir.

Pac. Let me perifh elfe. [*To Lelia.*]

Lel. You make me blufh Sir.

Pa. Let me die if any thing's more ferious.

Lyf. Come how is't joy?

Jul. Thank thee Deareft.

Lyf. The world may laugh, and names of fcorn invent,
　　But to be Cuckolds nothing it content.

A C T

ACT V. SCENE I.

Lysander.

Lys. Tis strange that we can fasten no such thing as honor upon the Sex, whereas a man's lies every where. Twinge him by the nose, his honour's there, and presently must be redeem'd.

Kick him, and 'tis remov'd to's backside, and must be engaged.

But this of woman-kind is really nothing. For if one unmarried chance to kick up her heeles, the reproach returns upon the family.

Or if a wife prove gamesome more than ordinary, shee's thought a wit, and cunning; and 'tis the husband's branded with the name of scorn.

Now should I go kill *Pisauro* to redeem my honour: and if I do, die honourably by an Executioner, or fly my Country: Or if I fall my self, they'l cry there died a silly cuckold, worth the while. I thank my stars I'me less nice in these points, and have found out a safer way.

Enter Juliana.

Welcome dearest, I was sending for thee.

Jul. I fear'd you might be angry.

Lys. What for such petty faults?

Jul. Nay now you speak as if you did not think me honest.

Lys. Not honest? Why you know I have no reason to the contrary: Prithee no more on't, I wou'd make a bargain with thee.

Jul. With me Sir? What do you mean?

Lys. In short, what is't you're willing to take a year for alimony?

Jul. This is harder than the first.

Lys. 'Tis that, that must be understood, for I resolve to carry on my part in the *Reformation* by this means. Consult

your

your felf and friends, for I would have you live in credit ftill.

Jul. Pray Sir be plain.

Lyf. Why thus.

Write me down fo much for cloaths, fo much for diet, and lodgings: fomething too for pleafure I'le allow; 'tis the faving Englifh way, and 'tis but reafonable when a wife proves falfe, fhe fhould be ftinted, and the overplus fhould keep a Mifs. Come, come, I'me out of my frollick humor now, and am ferious.

Jul. Now you are cruel, will you quite ruine me?

Lyf. No fuch matter, I'le be as civil too as any man, only retrench fome fmall fums you us'd to fpend in charitable ufes, as fourty pound to fuch a Nunnery, alias for a new fuit; twenty unto fuch a Monaftery, alias a new Wigg: why fhould you be lavifh in your good deeds? There's fcarce a Covent in the town but's bound to pray for you.

Jul. Pray pardon me, you us'd to fay you loved me.

Lyf. I pardon you with all my heart; but I'le take care that you fhall fin no more with my purfe, nor let *Pifauro* brave it with my wealth, as I know he does; come, it is in vain for to deny.

Jul. Nay if you grow angry once, *Emilia* does fo to; why fhould not I have the fame liberty?

Lyf. There are fome thirty and odd reafons to the contrary, befides the common practice; but that which muft fatisfie you is, I will not have it fo, and 'tis in my power to hinder it, remember what I fay.

[*Exit* Lyfander.

Enter Pifauro *and* Lelia.

Jul. Oh *Pifauro*, we're undone.

Pif. Come, no fuch matter, I have overheard it all, if *Pacheco* marry *Lelia*, as 'tis almoft out of doubt, this fore will foon be heal'd; befides my fortune's not fo very low, but I can live, and your allowance will be fair, I dare promife.

Jul. But will you ftill love me?

Pif. I'le double it if poffible.

Jul.

Jul. All that troubles me is, I shall want my wealth to serve you with.

Pif. Prithee no more, we lose time, *Lelia* be careful not to seem too coy, but if he comes to steal you let him carry off the prize: Friends, or the grave will soon reconcile *Camillo*: I must thither and see how affairs go, come courage Madam we can never want.

Jul. I fear nothing but losing my Gallant.

Lel. I'me resolv'd to make sure of mine.

[*Exeunt Omnes.*

Scena Secunda.

Pacheco, Tutor.

Pa. Am I exact in every thing? the colours suited? and my cloaths cut with the modish air?

Tut. To a thought: You see what 'tis to imploy a Taylor knowing in the fashion. There's nothing like your French cut Sir; you shall have a country Gentleman come to town, and throw away a years revenue on a suit on purpose to be laught at, hang me if a Livery been't more creditable.

Pac. Then there's much in the wearing of them too, why here now, what would this belt be valued at, without I wore it? Now it imploys the hands, and gives a grace to all the gate.

Tut. I joy to see you thus improved, you may read to me shortly. Oh dear Pupil.

Pac. Then there's the cock of the hat, tying of the shirt, fashions of crevats, the wearing of a Wig that's friz'd or curl'd, things that alter daily, and that these poor fools can ne're pretend to.

Tut. You amaze me Sir, I shall grow proud of my success.

Pa. Take me if I had not rather pass a judgment of a man, from a shake *a la mode*, wearing of a Mistresses faver, or the tying of a knot (there's a perfect Genius shown in that) than from a months converse.

Tut.

Tut. You have reason Sir; these are the things men tra-vel for, trust me you may be a pattern to the very Author of the fashion. Nay if you're once resolved I know you must needs carry her, but----

Pa. No more objections good *Tutor.*

Tut. Not I Sir, I see she's fair, believe her vertuous and a fortune, but yet----

Pa. More but's yet? now I begin to think thou envieft me, 'tis certain I will do something shall make me chief; truth is, *Lysander* bid fair for the command, but at the last I've found it, and defie him, and all the rest, to think of Con-quest.

Tut. May I know it?

Pa. Yes on condition you'l not speak a word to hinder my design.

Tut. Since you are so resolute I engage.

Pa. Then thus. I will to *Lelia* thus drest as I am, which certainly must do't, and without the least enquiry after for-tune, or consent of friends marry her for love; the height of Gallantry, and top of *Reformation*, hah?

Tut. I may Sir.

Pach. Not a word.

Tut. I may go with you Sir.

Pac. No, I'le have the honor of the action my self, when I return expect me conqueror.

Tut. No doubt of that, you'l find but little opposition.

Pac. I can but think when 'tis done what pleasures I shall have, and blest occasions of new words; As, my Joy, my chuck, my dear, my sweet honey-comb, and she answers in as good a stile; for I resolve to teach her all the English words. Adieu.

[*Exit* Pacheco.

Tut. Send you a fair wind, I've gold depends upon your good success.

Enter Pisauro.

Pis. Well met *Tutor*, where's *Pacheco*? we must not let him cool.

Tut

Tut. There's no fear: he juſt now left me, with a Reſolution to conclude before he will return.

Piſ. Then we're happy: his ſwearing of *Lyſander* was unlucky.

Tut. It muſt be pardon'd, 'twas perfect zeal and ignorance.

Antonio, Pedro, Mariana, Iſmena.

Ant. Save ye Gentlemen: what news from *Camillo, Tutor* ?

Tut. They were both faſt within this half hour.

Piſ. 'Tis much about the time they are to wake.

Mar. Shall we beg a favor from you then Sir ?

Tut. You may command it Madam.

Mar. 'Tis that you'd watch my Father, and give us notice when he ſtirs.

Tut. I fly to ſerve you.   [*Exit* Tutor.

Ant. 'Twas bravely carryed by *Lyſander.*

Ped. That, that pleas'd me was, he nickt the *Reformation* too.

Ant. To a thought : There if the women be diſpleaſed, 'tis but finding a pretence of quarrel, ſue their husbands, and the law gives them the thirds of the Eſtate to keep Gallants with.

Piſ. I can hardly recover my ſelf though I know I'me out of danger : I would have parted with the little of my Eſtate to any man breathing for a new Song.

Ant. Faith at the beſt 'twas but a leaſe, and that fairly forfeited to the Lord too.

Ped. What will you take for't now it's renew'd *Piſauro* ?

Piſ. Not renewed upon ſo good termes as you imagine ; but I'le not part with it, whilſt the ground bears any crop.

(To *Iſm.*) *Mar.* 'Tis ſtrange the very being women ſhould oblige us to diſſemble thus.

Iſm. You ſee 'tis true, for my part I do confeſs I love and would give all the world to marry my *Antonio.*

Mar I *Pedro.* Know 'tis the only remedy for our misfortunes, yet muſt not let them know it.

Ant. Fie Ladies not out of your fright yet !

Mar. Yes Sir we were talking of a greater danger; for
though

though I'me naturally devout, I don't love to fay my prayers on force.

Ifm. And though I have no hatred againſt mankind, yet to have one thruſt upon me thus, goes a little againſt the hair.

Ant. We have propoſed a way, that will prevent both dangers, would you follow it.

Ifm. I run the ſame hazard of a husband.

Mar. And I one worſe than that, of being Nun.

Ped. Why Madam, can you think it better to trifle time away in telling beads, and change your youth and briskneſs for Melancholy looks and wrinckles?

Ant. And you reſolve to ſigh away your life ſome three ſtories high, make complaints, and talk to the men it'h' Arras? That muſt be your fortune if you wed *Leandro.*

Ifm. Suppoſe all this true, how can you have the confidence to ask us for to marry you? Is it neceſſary we muſt break our necks to avoid drowning? Or to ſhun my fathers making us ſlaves go ſhackle up our ſelves?

Ant. As for liberty, you ſhall make your own propoſitions.

Mar. Which you will keep religiouſly until you've married us, and then break at pleaſure.

Ped. How can you imagine to avoid this danger?

Ifm. Pugh, that we'l think on when it comes, at preſent we are free.

Pif. But to be ſerious Ladies be your own Judges, is there not ſomething in the Society of men you much deſire?

Ifm. Confeſt, but ne're will purchaſe it at ſuch a rate as marriage.

Pif. Why then you muſt reſolve to be kind without it. 'Tis a hard caſe if you neither lead nor drive.

Ant. That we muſt be ſtretcht upon a rack, for no fault too, without the leaſt hope of eaſe.

Ifm. What can you deſire more than this freedom?

Ant. Very much: That is the very thing deſtroyes our hopes, were you but ſimpring, mimping, bridling Ladies, you were ſure prize; thoſe ſort of cattel are ſo little us'd to ſpeak, they think it modeſty not to deny you.

Pif. Or what do you think of a down demure look?

Ped. That never fails neither, I always challenge them, and what they mean for bashfulness, conclude a certain sign of guilt.

Ism. You're obliging Gentlemen, there's half womankind condemn'd already.

Ant. Then there's your devout souls, that sigh and whine, have something of Religion in their very gate; and never speak but in a tone of zeal and purity.

Pif. Pox on them, I must be hungry indeed to feed there, they are too common, and usually belong to a whole fraternity : If they can but learn to call their sins by new names, they pass for vertues ; and she that sins deepest is the truest Saint.

Ant. No, no, they're your brisk Ladies that are the hardest conquest. 'Tis true you give us so much freedom, we can't find confidence to ask more, yet when we cast it all up it signifies----just nothing.

Ped. Or if we do venture to ask, 'tis but lost labour, you'l never understand us, but wheadle't off with a laugh or some odd story.

Mar. Well Gentlemen we're beholden to you that our Honor's safe in your opinions.

Ped. And that acknowledgment is all the recompence we're like to have.

Mar. For all I can perceive Sir.

Pif. But consider a little : is there no little inclinations, no beatings here----Madam more than ordinary?

Ism. No Sir I can find no such matter.

Ant. But suppose that to your freedom I should offer that, which uses to be sweeter to your Sex, Revenge too?

Ism. Revenge would do something could I get shut of you once, but I swear you're grown so troublesome.

Ant. In short then, Madam, you resolve to lose both, desert the publick cause, and----

Ism. I have no natural in-bred hatred to your person; and Revenge does tempt a little. But----

Let

(69)

Let me die, if I can make objections, I shall hold out no longer. (*Aside.*)

Enter Antonio's Boy *in womans cloaths.*

Pis. Whom do you seek Lady?

Boy. *Antonio* Sir.

Ant. Your Servant Madam, hang me if I knew you at the first glance. Thou com'st luckily: be sure not to be amaz'd at whatsoe're I say or do, but answer me in my own strain.
[*Ant. kisses his hand.*]

Ism. Who is this? they're mighty well acquainted Sir methinks.

Pis. Faith Madam I can't guess, she's very fair.

Ism. But well: I know some Ladies will not be ashamed to shew their faces in her company. Would I could blast that little beauty that she has. (*Aside.*)

Ant. I thought our loves would ne're admit of jealousie, but thou art too kind. (*Aloud.*)

Boy. 'Tis you have made me so, I were ingrateful Sir indeed should I not endeavour to return your love.

(*Aside*) *Ism.* How's this? Return his love? then I am wretched.

Pis. You seem angry Madam.

Ism. Not I Sir, 'tis not in the power of man to make me so, (*Aside*) but that woman does.

(*Aloud*) *Boy.* You think me Sir too free I fear.

Ant. No dearest, our old love may challenge this and more.
Ism. May they poison thee. [*Salutes her*]

(*Aside*) *Ped.* I smell it, 'tis *Antonio*'s Boy he courts. And she must love by her concern. Now I'le strike home.

Ant. You have your story ready for *Camillo.*

Boy. Yes Sir.

(*Aloud*) *Ant.* And you'l not fail to meet me there Dearest?

Boy. I shall ne're deny my self a happiness.

(*To Ped.*) *Mar.* But are you sure my Sister will be found so easy as to yield?

Ped. I only beg the promise that you'l follow her example.

Mar. I may have confidence enough in her to grant,
and.

and yet shew little kindness. (*Aside*) at worst it saves my blushes.

Ped. That little's all I ask, Madam.

Ant. I'le only end a formal compliment or two.

(*Aside*) *Ism.* Treacherous base man!

Ant. Pisauro, shall I beg you would conduct this Lady?

Pis. You honor me with the trust.

[*Exeunt* Pisauro, Boy.

Ism. Will you go Sister?

Ant. You'l give me leave to wait on you Madam.

Ism. No Sir, you have your hands full I see already, and may spare your formal compliments. Would you fail your assignation with so great a beauty?

(*Aside*) *Ant.* As I could wish. She is not ugly Madam.

Ism. I don't intend a quarrel on the subject. 'Tis indifferent to me what she is.

Ant. I see it is Madam; nor could you blame me for courting her, when I found you so cruel.

Ism. I blame you? Why did you not leave Pisauro here, and go your self? there's no body so fond of your company. Come Sister. (to *Pedro*) I hope Sir you'l be so kind as to shew us the way home.

Mar. Nay fie Sister part friends. (to *Pedro*) You see Sir we are like to meet.

Ped. I'le take my fortune Madam, (*Aside*) and know I have a sure card to play.

Ant. 'Tis pretty to fall from the discourse of marriage into this of chiding.

Ism. Marriage? I'le rather be shut up with Leandro in a grave, than ever have a thought of you.

Ant. But I'me sure you will; more, know you must. Nay what is more yet, am confident 'twill be a match.

Ism. Now you're impudent. Did I ever shew the least kindness to you?

Ant. Confest, but this anger makes me think you have had no unkindness for me.

Ism. To vex you, I will confess it true, but add to it, that I hate you now.

Ant.

Ant. 'Tis very strange, all that you can say, can never make me believ't.

Ifm. I tell you I should hate my self, should I ever have the least good thought of you. Nay I shall hate all mankind for your sake, scarce spare my Brother for beginning our acquaintance.

Ant. This still confirms me more in my opinion.

Mar. This is mad courtship.

Ped. I know it must succeed, for nothing heightens love so much as a misgrounded jealousie.

Ant. What if I would promise, I would love no woman besides you ? is there no hopes of pardon ?

Ifm. No, I scorn it now.

Ant. If I swear I never did love a woman ?

Ifm. Nothing. I know it false, and if I doated on you, should hate you for this lie.

Enter Tutor.

Tut. Ladies, you must shift for yourselves, and that with speed : your Father is awake, has sent for *Leandro*; and to the Senate, that he may force you home, where e're he finds you.

Ped. You know your old retreat. *Ifm.* I'le die first.

Mar. And I'le be as good as my word, and follow my Sister.

Ant. Now I begin to find I'me wretched.

If this unlucky woman had not come I had been happy.

Ifm. And I more miserable far than now. Come Sister let's fly any whither from these men.

Ant. Pray stay Madam, since I have work't you to a height, and am confirm'd you love me by this jealousie, know that Lady was my Boy, drest in that habit to procure your liberty. I knew I had no other way to make this blest discovery. Will you yet give me leave ?

Ifm. I am worse angry than before to be betrai'd by this trick.

Ant. Consider Madam you'd better do't, I'le make good my promise, liberty and Revenge.

Ifm. No, no such matter : it may be I'le vouchsafe to hear your story out.

Tut. A minutes stay will ruine all.

Mar.

Mar. What do you resolve on Sister?

Ism. Only that I will not have *Leandro.*

Ped. My hopes are fair yet Madam.

Mar. You know the grounds on which they stand.

Tut. Away I say. I easily guess where this quarrel will end.   [*Exeunt Omnes.*

Enter Camillo, Leandro.

Cam. Never plead for them, to be made the talk and story of all the town, Sung in Ballads, for't will come to that ; The careful father gull'd, or old *Camillo*'s dream, I can, nor will hear no more.

Lean. Threatning will but make them fly your fury: whereas a promise of pardon brings them with submission into your power, and then you may contrive their punishment.

Cam. Contrive? do you hear me?

For the first I'le have a dungeon so dark and streight that she shall grope the way unto her mouth, and have no other air but sighs to live on. The second you should never wed, did I not believe you would invent some lasting terrors unto all that are or shall be Wives.

Lea. Trust me with that: but first it's necessary, I seek 'em out, and bring them home.

Cam. If they refuse, use force; the Senate cannot deny their power to so just designs.

Lea. I hope we shall not need it.

[*Exit* Leandro.

Cam. Never was man at my age so rid.

To be rock't asleep like a great Baby, whilst they are all a revelling. Well, I shall meet with these dap-chicks: That *Jay* my son, with the Owl his *Tutor,* and if I do----

Enter Boy, *in womans cloaths.*

Hah! who have we here?

Boy. You may wonder at a strangers rudeness Sir, and why a woman thus intrudes.

Cam. By my troth so I do, but the Divel's in you all for impudence.

Boy. When you know I have necessity and Justice on
my

my fide, I cannot doubt but you'l relieve my mifery.

Cam. A beggar in this garb! be gon, I have no time to hear long ftories, nor will to fupply your wants.

Boy. To relieve my wants will never make you poorer Sir.

Cam. The right religious Cant to? you know the way, be gon.

Boy. Pray hear me out, and then I know you will have pitty.

[Camillo *turns away, fhe kneels.*]

If e're you had a Mother, you owed a duty to, or wife you lov'd.

Cam. 'Tis a pretty tone this. [*turns away.*]

Boy. If you have daughters, as I knovv you have, whofe honor you'd preferve from ftain : if any thing that's yet more dear, by all I do conjure you to hear me out.

Cam. Now am I fuch a Coxcomb, that though I know it is a cheat, yet I muft liften, come rife and begin then.

Boy. This moft unhappy woman that you fee, whofe little beauty tears and grief have turn'd to ruins, yet was once thought fair, till perjury and all that's falfe (*weeps*) O falfe *Leandro* !

Cam. How! was't not *Leandro* that fhe nam'd? What can this mean?

Boy. Till he falfe man by force and treachery, had ravifht all my wealth, and left me thus neglected.

Cam. Come pray be plain, I'le hear you now with patience.

Boy. As foon as grief will let me Sir.

Cam. There's no truft in woman-kind if this be falfe.

Boy. My Father was a Merchant, and accounted rich, his place of living *Candy*, whilft alive, Heaven reft his foul.

Cam. This muft be true, it moves me too. His name?

Boy. *Fabricio.* When the enemy approacht our walls, he as commander for this State, and in their Services loft his life. 'Twas that unhappy minute, when I faw *Leandro* firft, whofe feeming goodnefs might have tempted one more wife, than miferable me.

Cam. Pray on. I long to hear thee out.

Boy. In fhort, my Mother trufted him with all concerns,

L   her

her wealth, her self, and me. He liv'd a while a faithful Guardian. And I (for it muft out) too foon lov'd.

Cam. Your name Lady?

Boy. *Fabia,* in a word.

He promis'd to convey our family, and riches to this town, did fo, but in the voyage, after a thoufand vows of Marriage, which we could not then confummate, ftole my honor, and ever fince hath left me to my grief. (*weeps.*)

Cam. Bleft difcovery, truft me now I pitty thee.

Boy. If you pitty, help me Sir and fave your felf, this fame *Leandro* ftill muft needs be falfe, and will you throw away a Virgin on a perjur'd man? And if fhe marries him, I'me loft for ever.

Cam. If I find this ftory true, I'le promife that your Father's name's *Fabritio,* your's *Fabia.*

Hold, I think I hear him coming.

Enter Leandro, Antonio, Pedro, Mariana, Ifmena.

Mar. Ifm. ⎫ Away, away, I have nothing to fay to you. Nor
kneel. ⎬ you neither, you may return.

Ant. We have bufinefs Sir that much concerns you.

Cam. Let it be what it will I have no leifure: if you will ftay, come not near my daughters, but go you to that corner of the room, you to this; fo the Divel's in you if you play tricks at this diftance. My bufinefs is with *Leandro.*

Lea. Your Pleafure Sir.

Cam. Only a little fcruple, I remember I have fworn, never to match my daughter with a man that had not hazarded his life to ferve the State.

Lea. That can be no Obftacle. I've ferv'd it long, and when our *Candy* was befieged, fent numbers of the infidels to feek their Prophet in the other world. This my friends can witnefs.

Cam. You knew *Fabritio* then?

(*Afide*) *Ant.* How it works?

Lea. *Fabritio* was my leader Sir, and train'd me up to Arms, many a bold fally has he made, and brought back Victory,

nor

nor did he tamely lose his life, but fell encompass'd with an host of slaughter'd enemies.

(*Aside*) *Cam.* Thus far we do agree. How fared it with his wife and daughter Sir? I have heard he left both.

Lea. He did, and both patterns to the Sex. They shar'd the common fortune, and when the town was yielded up set sail for *Venice*.

(*Aside*) *Cam.* Right yet.

How was the daughter call'd?

Lea. *Fabia.* (What can all this mean? (*Aside*.)

(*Aside*) *Cam.* I am confirm'd.

Do you know this Lady?   [*points to the* Boy.]

Lea. No Sir, nor till this minute ever saw her face.

Boy. O Perjur'd man! is *Fabia* so soon forgot? false, false *Leandro.*

Cam. Pray look again.

Lea. May I ne're enjoy the thing I love on earth, or when I die heaven----

(*Aside*) *Cam.* His strong denials make me confident. Consider once again, is not this *Fabia*?

Fabia whom you have wrong'd?

Lea. Neither Sir if you require oaths.

Boy. If oaths could have obliged, I never had become thus wretched.

Lea. Heavens, that e're such impudence should wear the shape of women! wer't thou not so----

Cam. Come, no threats Sir.

She's in a sanctuary in my house. Take her, and make amends for all your former injuries.

Lea. What injuries? you will distract me Sir, give me but a minute for to clear my self.

Cam. No, I am satisfied already, and will not be cheated, nor let my daughter run her self to certain ruine. I'le in, and fetch the writing you have given.   [*Exit* Camillo.

Lea. Hell and Furies.

Ant. Save you Sir, how do you like your Island?

Lea. Will you never leave your tortures?

Ped. This is the hell we told you of, if you ventured to sin again.

Ant. As for your new discovery I have taken possession, and it's like to be call'd by my name; in short I am married to *Ismena*, *Pedro* to *Mariana*, and this *Fabia* is the *Boy* drest up to amuse *Camillo*.

Ped. Here take him, you're so much an *Italian*, you need not lose your Mistrifs.

Lea. You shall find me more by my Revenge.

[*Exit* Leandro.

Ant. Thus far our plot succeeds.

Boy, do you steal away and get undrest: I would not have *Camillo* find that cheat yet. [*Exit* Boy.

Mar. He's coming: To our places.

Enter Camillo *with writings.*

Cam. Here, here, where's *Leandro* ?

Mar. Gone Sir.

Cam. And *Fabia* ?

Mar. Yes Sir but not together.

Cam. Then these must be sent.

Now I have leisure to come to you, Runagates, for though you have escaped this danger, you must not think to go free. I have provided for ye both, 'tis not your powder that can find another remedy, I will not eat nor drink till it's perform'd. I guess your business Gentlemen, but you may spare your pains.

Enter Pacheco, Lelia, Pisauro, Juliana.

Cam. What can this prove ?

Pacheco
Lelia *kneel.* } We kneel for blessing Sir.

Cam. I give it you; but who's this ?

Pac. Your Daughter, whilst I call her wife.

Cam. Still more wretched? Go fool thou hast undone thy self; and shalt live nor pittied nor relieved by me.

That I should ever be a Father !

But I'le study to forget the name.

Thefe

Thefe a Nunnery if poffible fhall fave from ruine. In Hay.

Ant.⎫
Ped.⎬ That we forbid Sir.

Cam. What fhall I not rule my own family in my own houfe? In I fay.

Ant. They may with juftice difobey, they leave their husbands here.

Ant. Who thus in duty ask your bleffing.

Cam. Bleffing? e'ne the down-right Divel take you all, I am gull'd, cheated, fool'd.   [*Exit* Camillo.

Mar. Oh Pedro, vve can never profper if a fathers bleffing be denied.

Ped. Never fear Madam, a little patience reconciles all.

Enter Lyfander, Tutor.

Lyf. Joy Gallants. Three vveddings in a day? the State can never vvant Souldiers.

Pac. There's little joy belongs to me. The *Reformation* goes on too faft novv; for though I like this marrying for love, I hate this damn'd Englifh vvay of difinheriting.

Lyf. What can this mean?

Ant. Nay faith the old Gentleman's ftrangely angry, prithee try vvhat you can do *Lyfander*, your acquaintance has been great.

Lyf. I vvill, I'me confident vvhen once he knovvs your qualities, he'l think his daughters vvell beftovv'd, and an only Sons pardon is foon obtain'd.   [*Exit* Lyfander.

Ifm. However it fucceed, I'de rather run a thoufand dangers than be flave to *Leandro*'s jealoufie. This vvas a brave revenge done like a Mafter of your Art.

Ant. That part of my promife is fulfill'd then; but novv't's too late to bargain for your liberty, you're at my mercy ftill.

Ifm. I thought it beft to truft you.

I knevv a promife vvas fooner broke, than your good nature turn'd.

Ant. Hovvever of my ovvn accord I here ingage to be true, until I find you falfe, and then I'le take *Lyfander*'s pattern.

Ifm. Then here I promife for you, that you alvvays fhall
be

be true. I ever lov'd the talk of liberty, more than the thing it self.

Ped. You *Mariana*, may challenge all the freedom that you'l take.

Mar. I shall take the less, for your giving me so much.

Enter Nurse *just awake.*

Nurse. I have found my tongue again, and if I don't rail you all deaf----

Ped. Say you so, I have the other gag for you.

[*Exit* Nurse.

Pis. Pray Gentlemen, reckon it a considerable piece of *Reformation*, that we have found out two infallible remedies, to cure an old womans talking.

Enter Lysander.

Ant. How is't? where is he?

Lys. He's come unto himself again, now he considers who you are, and follows me.

(*Enter* Jul.) Well met Madam, I hope you're pleas'd.

Jul. Since you are so cruel as to part, I must allow you truly noble.

Lys. I doubt *Pisauro* some of these fine feathers must molt.

Pis. You're deceived Sir, with these I intend to purchase a rich wife, and pay some of my old scores to *Juliana*.

Enter Camillo.   [*They kneel.*

Cam. Heaven bless you; and if you can live on that, do. But I am so much a Reformer, as not to part with a farthing of money, without settlement, Gentlemen.

Ant. That shall never breed a difference.

Cam. I knew your Father well *Antonio*; if you prove as well, my daughter's happy.

Your's *Pedro*, for so I'me told you're cal'd, is my peculiar friend, and if he likes the match, I will do any thing that's just.

(*To* Pac.) But what can you pretend to, with your Gimcracks and travels, hah?

Pac. I married Sir for love and Virtue, and have heard you say it was your fault (if it may be accounted one) when

when you took my Mother ; I only follow'd your example.

Tut. Well nick't Pupil.

Cam. H'as found my weak fide, it muſt not be denied. Well, you ſhall be upon your good behavior.

Aſide {*Pac.* If it comes to that I know I ſhall ſoon win him.
{*Tut.* I'le give you Lectures for't to morrow.

(To *Piſ.*) My gold's good Sir.

Piſ. Yes this little Pinnace ſailes to fetch it home. }
Lel. And will bring it too, I'le warrant you.   } *Aſide.*

Cam. Come you ſhall all dine with me, we will be ſo long friends at leaſt.

If two of theſe adventures come off well, I have made a ſaving voyage.

Ant. I have ſomething to do ſtill, which is the Reforming of you Mounſieur *Tutor.* Nay never ſhrink, for one of theſe things muſt be ſubſcribed to, either chuſe to renounce your intereſt in the Society.

Tut. That's hard.

Ant. Or your pretence to Poetry, and acquaintance with the Muſes as you call't.

Tut. Harder yet.

Ant. Or engage in three months, to produce a Play which ſhall have nothing in't borrow'd, nor improbable, nor prophane, nor bawdy.

Tut. This is almoſt impoſſible, but yet I'le venture, and if my Play miſcarries here, ſet ſail for *England*, where any one of theſe qualities will make it famous.

Ped. Now it's perfect, *Antonio.*

We're married, yet can know no jealouſie.

Mar. And Siſter we are wives, and yet are free.

Ant. Bleſt *Reformation!*

All's right, we ſhould have nothing left to do,
Could we Reform one Engliſh cuſtom too,
That's the damn'd trade of cenſuring in you.

F I N I S.

EPILOGUE.

(Spoken by Mr. *Smith*.)

HOw do you like our Reformation now?
Come, we're amongst our selves. Here are Wits too. *pointing to Pacheco and Tutour.*
Or shall's to th' Coffee-house and there debate,
Each take his Chair and Pipe and judg in State?
Lord how they wait a Wit that's fam'd in Town!
He lookes about him with a scornful frown,
Then picks his Favourite out and sits him down.
Take me how is't? Have you seen our new Play?
Yes faith, and how? a half Crown thrown away,
Pox on't he cries, I Droll'd and Slept it out;
'Twas some Raw Fop: Then proudly stares about;
Then shrugs and whispers, laughs, then swears aloud.
The whilst there's silence kept by all the Croud.
At length he nods and cocks, is heard to say,
D--- me 'tis true, and thus he damns the Play,
Rises, lookes big and combs, then goes his VVay.
'Tis strange to think how absolute they are,
VVhen lookes, half VVords and Oathes, destroy or spare.
VVe can expect no favour; these are known
Foes unto every thing that's not their own.
And rather too, than that shall want applause,
They'l clap themselves and that way gain the cause.
By such like Arts they rule the stage and you,
And what was Favour first, now claim as due.
For shame use your Authority and free
Your selves from these usurpers Tyranny,
Ne're wait their censure more, but let them know
You have the power that they pretended to.
They wheadle you to clap bad plays they write:
To be reveng'd do you clap this to night.
But Ladies you our Author hopes to find
In your own Cause and for your own sakes kind,
Since 'tis the first design of's Poetry
Both how to gain and give you Liberty.